AF564449

# BOOK PUBLISHING MANAGEMENT

BY THE SAME AUTHOR

*Authors and Publishers*

# BOOK PUBLISHING MANAGEMENT

G. S. Jolly

First Published: 2009

Published by Ashok Gosain and Ashish Gosain for
HAR-ANAND PUBLICATIONS PVT LTD
E-49/3, Okhla Industrial Area, Phase-II, New Delhi-110020
Tel: 41603490 Fax: 011-41708607
E-mail: haranand@rediffmail.com
Website: www.haranandpublications.com

Printed in India at Ram Book Binding House.

# Preface

Publishing is among the most fascinating and rewarding human activities. It helps in giving shape, in the form of a book, to the ideas and thoughts of a writer as a result of creative or acquired knowledge. Book publishing in India is on the throes of major convulsions. These have been brought about primarily by explosion in the field of education going on unabated since independence.

The vendor landscape in India presents an interesting picture offering a range of publishing out-sourcing services. While smaller players predominantly offer data conversion/digitisation services, larger players offer the entire range including design, content development, data conversion and even turnkey project management services to their clients.

The demand for trained personnel in the field, therefore, has grown many folds. The book is an attempt to outline the procedures of book publishing. The main emphasis is on the functioning of various departments to give a holistic view of what happens in book publishing.

The book should serve as a practical guide and reference to budding professionals in this field and provide assistance in understanding at all levels of various processes of book publishing. This should be of special interest to academicians who wish to publish themselves, book editors, librarians and all those interested in the world of books.

The book is planned for study and reference for the students of Post Graduate Diploma Courses of various prestigious universities and institutions. The various themes discussed in the publication provide an insight into various topics, which form part of the syllabi of various professional courses in book publishing, printing, and mass communication, Journalism etc.

The book has been divided in five parts. Each part describes a different aspect of book publishing process thus giving an understanding of the entire working of a publishing House.

Part one attempts to present bird's eye view of history of publishing in India and gives a detailed narrative of the functioning of various departments of a publishing house. It will help readers to understand the various jobs performed in a publishing house and appreciate the importance of each one in the production of a book.

Part two deals with the role the editorial department plays in creation of a manuscript, which is clear, well organized and consistent in style and exposition. It will help readers to recognize the importance of the editor in the process of book publishing.

Transforming a loosely written manuscript into a finished book is the job of the production department. Part three highlights the processes of printing and, the importance of paper, binding and new technologies which have revolutionised the traditional methods of book production.

The process of publishing completes only after the book reaches the hands of the readers. What ways and means a publishing house, to reach the potential buyers adopts, is the essence of part four of this book. It highlights the role of the sales a promotion department of a publishing house.

Part five of the book essays to explain the business economics of book publishing and introduces the role and significance of International Standard Book Number, the issues of copyright and understanding the publisher's contract.

The work could not have been completed without the unflinching support of my publisher Mr. Narendra Kumar. I am deeply grateful to him.

My special thank to my wife for inspiring me to write this work.

G. S. JOLLY

# Contents

# Part I
# An Overview of Book Publishing

# 1
# Publishing in India—Retrospect and Prospect

Publishing is among the most fascinating and rewarding human activities. It helps in giving shape, in the form of a book, to the ideas and thoughts of a writer as a result of creative or acquired knowledge. Book publishing in India is on the throes of major convulsions. These have been brought about primarily by explosion in the field of education going on unabated since independence.

It is a matter of great satisfaction and pride for the Indian publishing fraternity that India has been chosen as the Guest of Honour at the Frankfurt Book Fair to be held in October 2006. It is the first time in the history of the Book Fair that a country has been conferred this honour in a span of 20 years, the first being in 1986. India has become a country to reckon with in the international world of publishing.

## THE PRESENT SCENARIO

India has truly arrived on the international publishing scene. There are more than 16000 publishers publishing 74000 books. Exports now comprise a healthy Rs. 4.6 billion compared to the paltry Rs. 330 millions in 1991. India ranks the third largest book producing country in English language.

India's Rs. 80 billion book publishing industry is riding a wave of success thanks to innovative marketing strategies like blog discussions, email to readers and preview booklets to promote new titles. Publishing in India has now become more globalised and integrated. Foreign direct investment in print media has made India a sought after destination for foreign players.

According to the latest University Grants Commission's 2005 statistics, there are 343 universities, 16885 colleges, 460,000 teachers and 9,953,000 students. The number has further swollen in the past two years. The growth and pattern of indigenous publishing is indicative of self sufficiency, as in every walk of life. University Grants Commission, the apex monitoring body of higher education in the country has approved Rs. 1,269.80 crore budget for the year 2006-2007 which is more than Rs. 495 crore more than the last year. This is a clear indication the treatment which higher education is being given in the present scenario.

Subsidiary status of Indian publishers, as adjunct of foreign publishing firms, is a story of the past. The industry is being professionalized to the extent that has resulted in foreign publishing giants making a bee line in starting their operations in India, either on their own or in collaboration with the Indian partners.

*History:* Publishing and printing in India has a long history dating back to sixteenth century. The origin of printing and publishing in India can be traced to a Jesuit Missionary who was responsible for printing first book in India with movable type in 1557. The title of the book was *Doctrine Christian.* Interestingly fifty nine years after the landing of Vasco da Gama, the first printing press was established in 1556. Within a hundred years of printing of Gutenberg's Bible in Germany, India initiated its groping towards fashioning of types for the many Indian languages.

In the following years printing presses by Christian missionaries were found dotting the coastline of the Indian peninsula. Goa, Cochin, Punnaikkayal and Ambalakkadu near Trichur were the places along the West coast and Tranquebar, Madras, Fort William Calcutta and Serampore along the East coast, represented the shaping of Indian printing.

Though the start of printing in Goa and its spread along the southern coast and its maturity at Tranquebar and Madras has been described as the dawn of printing, the sunrise in all its brilliance is attributed to William Carey, a shoe maker turned printer/publisher who bought a wooden printing press at a cost of £40, an amount which he received from his friend. The press, when reached Madanbati by boat in 1798, it was hailed by Carey and his coworkers and christined as 'Sahebdar Thakur' (diety of the whites). William Carey established his press in Serarmpore. During the next 31 years 2,12,000 items in 40 different languages were issued from the press.

With the rise of the British power, missionary efforts exploited the printing presses increasingly. Though printing had come to India as early as 1577, the tempo and output of the presses increased only after the British rule established itself.

Repeal of press laws by Charles Metcalfe was a turning point in the history of Indian printing and publishing. His belief that 'if India could be preserved as part of the British Empire only by keeping its inhabitants in a state of ignorance, our domination would be a curse to the country and ought to cease' led Charles Metcalfe to repeal the Press Acts. The removal of obnoxious press laws liberated the Indian press and opened the floodgates of printing in India for native publishers.

*Renaissance:* As a result of cultural renaissance in Bengal, books had begun to appear in vernacular languages. Cultural figures like Rabindera Nath Tagore, Bankim Chandra Chatterjee used books to press the Bengali cultural renaissance in the nineteenth century.

While few established publishers emerged at this time, books were circulated to the growing literate middle class in Bengal. Similar currents were present in other parts of the country. Yet this awakening did not see the emergence of publishing houses in the modern sense of the term. Individuals and organisations arranged for publishing of books, which made their way gradually to the target users. This was an inefficient means of dissemination of information, but the number of readers was small and concentrated in urban areas.

## RETROSPECT

The stress on the spread of education gave big boost to publishing activity in India. The demand for books and other reading material grew manifold.

Among the first publishers to take advantage of the growing need were British owned firms. Accordingly, Macmillan opened their office in 1903, followed by Longman in 1906. Oxford University Press started its operations in 1912. They were mainly concentrating their activities on importing foreign books and distributing them among the students of Indian schools and colleges. Since Indian schools and colleges largely followed the British system of education, most of the books could be adopted for Indian use without any alterations. Only occasionally, they ventured into publishing original books related to India.

*National Movement:* The Indian national movement gave an impetus to another crop of publishers who brought out political booklets and pamphlets. In this connection the name of G.A. Natesan of Madras can be taken as of a pioneer who reflected and propagated the cause of Indian nationalism through various publications, documentary studies and biographies.

The period between the world wars and just prior to independence, Indian publishing may be said to have emerged from a period of gainful experience. During this period general publishing, particularly political publishing, took the front Seat. Though much that was published during these years was political pamphleteering, it helped .a great deal in clarifying the issues and mobilising public opinion in favour of national movement and also providing the background for the growth of Indian publishing after independence.

Notable among those who dedicated themselves to Indian political publishing were Padma Publications, who published an intensely topical booklet-*Quit India,* giving Gandhiji's celebrated Quit India speech. Hind Kitabs published books of Indian interest including fiction. Kitabistan of Allahabad made its mark by publishing Indian editions of Jawaharlal Nehru's books. Peoples Publishing House was set up by then newly legalised Communist Party of India.

Renaissance Publishers was established by followers of M.N. Roy to assist in the dissemination of his political views. Bhartiya Vidya Bhavan also started its paperback series on topics of religious and spiritual interests.

Most of these early Indian publishers did not last long. Misrepresentation of the market due to largely political motivation of the publishing houses, harassment by British authorities, lack of professional and business expertise and experience and inadequate financial resources came in the way of success of these publishing houses. These pioneers did prove, however, that indigenous publishing of serious nature was possible and this helped to stimulate efforts made by the post independence publishers.

*Independence:* Indian publishing blossomed only after India attained independence. The spread of education and increase in literacy rate, opening of new universities and colleges, phenomenal increase in number of students, created an unprecedented demand for books.

Asia Publishing House which was founded in 1943 dominated the Indian publishing scene for almost two decades after independence. With a number of years experience behind it and with a powerful and expanding organisation for promotion and sale of its agency publications and with wider and valuable contacts in learned institutions, Asia Publishing House grew rapidly as an independent Indian publishing house of national standing that soon gained international status.

By 1973 it had published more than 4300 titles. But its significance in Indian publishing is not by the number of titles, but the standards it set in Indian publishing which made Indian books representative of editorial strength and production standards in international publishing.

History of societies, institutions and individuals is identifiable through specific landmarks along the road of time. Trends in Indian publishing similarly are to be divided into periods. One such phase in the post independence publishing is post Emergency period beginning March 1977.

## EMERGENCY AND AFTER

The Emergency 1975-1977 proved to be a catalyst for Indian publishing. It changed the pace of Indian publishing and brought it at par with publishing in any other country in terms of number of copies sold of a title. Before this phase, books on current affairs with exception here and there, were normally intended for specialists, limited to sale of edition of 2000 copies and that too extending over a period of several years.

Books on Emergency entered every drawing room. Publishing world thus discovered new group of readership. These books became Indian answers to American bestsellers. This phase revealed a new trend that the publishing is not only for the elite readers and library system of the country. Books became the items of mass consumption. The publishing houses who made their mark in this phase, include Hind

Pocket Books, Vision Books, Allied Publishers and above all, Vikas Publishing House.

Vikas, under its then Managing Director, Narendra Kumar, made a history of sorts. Narendra Kumar's vision of aggressive selling, use of unconventional promotion techniques and author's involvement in book promotion, gave him a Mida's touch. He successfully churned out best sellers one after the other like *The Judgement, Two Faces of Indira Gandhi, All the Prime Minister's Men.* More than a lakh copies of each individual titles were sold. A figure till then unheard of in Indian Publishing history.

*Subsidy Schemes:* While Indian publishers were gradually building up their lists there came a major development which had far reaching effect on the Indian publishing scene. This came in the shape of foreign subsidy schemes for providing low priced text-books to Indian students. First among those was E.L.B.S. of the British Government followed by Joint Indo-US Textbook Programme under which 1500 titles were printed and published in India and were made available to students at a price which was almost 1/5 of the original American edition. A similar Indo-Soviet Joint Textbook Programme was also launched in 1965.

These schemes had their blessings and blights. A local book industry is needed, no matter how great the availability of books from abroad. This is necessary for cultural enrichment, for self expression by the nation's thinkers, writers and artists for development of sense of national unity as well as of a sense of historic traditions. Foreign books may be useful in many ways for some readers. But for most of the book readers in most countries, the books must grow out of local soil.

It was realised that image of cultural heritage of any country can be best preserved by its own publishers and that textbooks should emanate from and reflect the country in which they are used. As a result of this, National Book Trust started its own subsidy scheme for publication of college level textbooks.

The soul of a country can be manifested only in the writings of its own language. Development of language is necessary because freshness and originality and real expression come only from the mother tongue. In India, publishing is done in twenty four regional languages. In order to give encouragement to Indian language publishing, government should play a vital role by reducing postal and freight rates on transportation of books, publicise Indian languages, provide low interest long term loans, make paper available at reasonable price and build library movement.

*Nationalisation of Textbooks:* The single largest segment of Indian publishing scene is educational publishing which includes textbooks, reference books and other supplementary reading materials at school and college level.

There are now more than 350 universities. The number of colleges have grown, from 933 in 1947 to around 20,000 in 2007. The student population at all stages in India is running in crores. The figure underlines the importance which school textbook publishing occupies in India. It is an accepted fact that publication of school textbooks provides the much needed constant fund flow to the publishers which also provides the base for supporting those books which the society needs but may not be financially sustainable.

The policy of nationalisation of school textbooks has taken the bread and butter away from the publishers and they have been made to eat crums alone. Primary, secondary and higher secondary textbooks have been nationalised and are being published by the agencies of the government. At national level N.C.E.R.T is playing an important role of producing and distributing the school textbooks. In some states the departments of education and textbook boards look after this activity.

The nationalisation scheme has certain inherent defects. According to an estimate more than 200 million textbooks are produced by different state publishing agencies making it difficult to reach out to students in time. Authors have been deprived of freedom of expression. Politicisation has acted counter to the objective of uniform education and national interest. Export potential of textbooks is not fully exploited.

## PROSPECT

It is a matter of great satisfaction and pride for the Indian publishing fraternity that India has been chosen as the Guest of Honour at the Frankfurt Book Fair held in October 2006. It is the first time in the history of the Book Fair that a country has been conferred this honour in a span of 20 years, the first being in 1986. India has become a country to reckon with in the international world of publishing.

India has truly arrived on the international publishing scene. There are more than 16000 publishers publishing 74000 books. Exports now comprise a healthy Rs. 4.6 billion compared to the paltry Rs. 330 millions in 1991. India ranks the third largest book producing country in English language.

Publishing in India has now become more globalised and integrated. Foreign direct investment in print media has made India a sought after destination for foreign players. Diversification and concentration of multinational multimedia corporations and ability to meet the local demands and cultural needs is what is expected of Indian publishing today. And the industry is fully geared to meet these challenges.

Economically, India is flabbergasting. This has been the theme of discussions at the World economic Forum in Devos. Indian publishing can be said to have come of age. Indian presence at the Devos was visibly felt because India has been the fastest growing free market economy of the world. India with its capabilities is roaring not only in its BPO (Business Process Outsourcing) industry but also KPO (Knowledge Processing Outsourcing) industry. In the area of outsourcing business process Indian companies were perceived to be delivering 'beyond cost gains with innovation and creative solutions'. India is fast becoming a credible investment destination and business partner.

India is today uniquely positioned to be a back-office support provider for the printing and publishing industry worldwide. A large population having good knowledge of English, rapidly falling costs of technology and communications, and its location in a time zone that can serve both the east and west in an ideal manner, have made India the country that many companies are turning to outsource their publishing activity.

*Export:* India's Rs. 80 billion book publishing industry is riding a wave of success, thanks to innovative marketing strategies like blog discussions, email to readers and preview booklets to promote new titles.

Export of print job has grown from 123 million in 1999 to 942 million in 2003. Out-sourcing in Indian publishing segment has been prevalent for more than three decades now. Macmillan began its off-shoring unit in India way back in 1977. According to Value Notes Data Base Pvt. Ltd., Indian off shoring in publishing vertical is expected to touch US $1.1 billion by 2010. According to the Value Notes research report, 'the major drivers of out-sourcing to India include the domestic English publishing industry with a more than 100 years history, the trained workforce, proficient in English language and publishing and significant cost arbitrage'.

The vendor landscape in India presents an interesting picture offering a range of publishing out-sourcing services. While smaller players predominantly offer data conversion/digitization services, larger players offer the entire range including design, content development, data conversion and even turnkey project management services to their clients.

The publishing outsourcing industry in India is poised for significant growth. The Indian BPO (Business process outsourcing) industry includes basic data and market research, equity research, management, engineering design, animation and simulation, medical content and services and education and publishing. India as a major KPO (Knowledge Processing Outsourcing) player in the world has inherent advantages because of its intellectual and Internet resource. The resulting economic success of the BPO industry has taken many firms to take their advanced knowledge work to off shore destinations.

*Electronic Edge:* With the introduction of electronic age book publishing will consist of combination of paper based publishing and publishing based on storage of information by electronic devices and techniques. There is, therefore, need to harness new inventions to the production of books in a cost effective manner and also to utilize their considerable powers in the management of publishing process and for the promotion and efficient distribution of the books produced. The new technologies would thus constitute an opportunity rather than a threat to book publishing.

The electronic edge has added new dimensions to publishing and printing. The computer, the microcomputer, word processor and all other sophisticated devices and accessories such as Desk Top Publishing, Windows etc., inspire and challenge the publishing to reach the pinnacle of perfection.

The electronic age has revolutionised the methods of printing, publishing and distribution of books and journals. Authors have now begun preparing manuscripts electronically, using word processors, freeing themselves from the tedium of preparing a handwritten or typed manuscript and has made additions and revisions easy and manageable. Nowadays, authors use floppy disks, CDs books are directly composed with page layout at Page Maker and other composing systems.

In the words of Vishwanath, the celebrated Indian publisher, "Indian publishing has survived through rough weathers and stormy seas because of the fighting will of committed and dedicated publishers who have strong instinct for survival in them. The future of publishing is bright for those who have the initiative and imagination."

The fear that the printed word might become obsolete in the electronic age is unfounded. It is impossible for it to happen. Of all the mankind's diverse tools undoubtedly the most astonishing are his books. If books were to disappear, history would disappear. So would men. Because if books are not life then what, is?

# 2

# Book Publishing and Structure of a Publishing House

Books are carriers of knowledge and cultural values in human society. They serve both national development and enrichment of human life. They foster better understanding between peoples and strengthen the desire for peace in the minds of men.

Books in one form or the other were always there since ancient days. The clay tablets of Mesopotamia and papyrus rolls of ancient Egypt, the first century parchment pages bound on one side known as Codex, the religious works produced during the middle ages, were the various manifestations of the book.

The introduction of paper and invention of movable type in the mid fifteenth century, made possible the printing of multiple copies of books and this method spread with great rapidity throughout the world.

In the eighteenth century, books made substantial progress and encyclopedia such as Britannica was published. Paper bound books made their mark in the nineteenth century and in the twentieth century, books became all prevalent and have entered all walks of human life.

## WHAT IS A BOOK

In its widest sense, a book is a body of material capable of being inscribed upon in some fashion, whether or not inscription has occurred. Therefore, any group of pages or leaves, bound or unbound and also any scroll or related group of writing tablets of any material would be called a book.

In a more precise way a book may be defined as a 'written work of substantial proportion, printed and bound in a unit of one or more volumes.'

UNESCO definition of a book is that 'a book is a non periodical printed publication of at least 49 or more pages exclusive of covers.'

The limit of 49 pages was prescribed by UNESCO for maintaining statistics of publications, otherwise, nations differ with regard to number of pages that can constitute a book.

The Concise Oxford Dictionary defines a book as 'a portable printed work filling a number of sheets fastened together in a cover.' Webster American Dictionary describes it as 'a set of written, printed or blank sheets bound together into a volume.'

The following systematic definition of a book has been worked out by Samuel Israel, which helps us distinguishing book from other print media like newspapers, posters, folders etc. It says, "A book is a series of sheets of paper, mostly of uniform size, bearing either text or illustrations or both, placed in a desired logical sequence, held firmly together (bound) at one edge in a manner that facilitates its viewing, reading and reference. And that its multiple copies are reproduced by mechanical photographic and other non-manual processes."

## FUNCTIONS OF A BOOK

What does a book do? The basic function of book is to educate. Education is the basis of all development and most essential factor in human progress. Books are essential tool for preserving and diffusing the world's storehouse of knowledge. Books are carriers and disseminators of ideas. They are most permanent, reasonable and extensive repository of the thoughts of civilised mankind.

Books have also been called the most efficient and most effective instrument of transfer of learning. Knowledge derived from books is most enduring and more permanent and sustainable than that obtained from other mass media.

Communication is an other function of the book. Books inform, educate and entertain. Books like other vehicles of information and sources of entertainment can change, influence, elevate, demean, exalt or depress those who expose themselves to them.

## WHAT IS PUBLISHING

The process of preparing the work of an author in the most suitable form and manner and presenting it in the most efficient manner to the widest possible audience is called publishing. Literally speaking, to publish means to make public, to send forth among the people—the words and pictures that creative minds of authors have produced, that editors have worked over, that printers have produced.

It is a process to make public, *i.e.* disseminating, either information or views, or literary, scientific or artistic creations. Publishing in general implies to prepare and make available written material for sale or distribution to the general public; while the term often refers to the printed material, new technologies allow work to be published without being formally composed or printed, as when a work is photocopied from type script and distributed or to be distributed without words either appearing on paper, or when a work is composed and available solely on electronic networks. More popularly, publishing means to release written work to the general public.

Publishing can also be defined as a series of processes involving many people inside and outside the publishing house, lasting at least a couple of months to a couple of years, before a loosely written manuscript delivered by an author is transformed into a book that can be sold or distributed.

It is the whole intellectual and business procedure of selecting and arranging to make a book and promoting its ultimate use. Publishing is both business and cultural activity. Books are vehicles of ideas, instruments of knowledge and storehouse of education but the task of bringing them into existence and of purveying them to their readers is a commercial activity requiring all the resources of head and heart of an entrepreneur.

The power of books is heavily dependent upon the judgement, integrity, taste and acumen of those who select, produce and market books—The publishers.

## WHO IS A PUBLISHER

Publisher is one who undertakes overall entrepreneurial responsibility for the publication of works, whether financing the publication of those works as an individual or an organisation. Therefore, an individual or institution can be a publisher. The main function of a publisher is to supply books to the world. With author on one side and readers on the other, a publisher serves as a link between the two.

According to UNESCO Standard a publisher is one who brings out at least four books, in a year. But an entrepreneur has to undergo the same process of publishing whether one book is published or four or more books are published in a year.

In the process of making the author's work available to the readers, the publisher occupies the central position. It is he who receives the manuscript, applies the editorial skills, prepares it for the press, converts it into a finished book with the help of printer, binder and suppliers of other raw materials required for producing the book and makes efforts to reach the intended market and consumers of the book. In other words a person or organisation who prepares the work of an author in the most suitable form and manner and presents to the widest possible audience is called a publisher. It is, therefore, he who by his judgement, taste, vision and business sense shapes not only the industry but also the literary and general culture of the society.

In fulfulling this objective, a publisher should constantly strive for better and enduring literature as against short term profits. A publisher who constantly disrespects the demand for quality and worth in the manuscripts despite temporary success will find his enterprise dying of spiritual starvation in the end. Just as a publisher who consistently ignores the commercial needs of the establishment will find, before long, that his cultural opportunities are negated by bankruptcy.

It is generally believed that a publisher who thinks right for posterity, thinks wrong for his balance sheet. Publishing is both cultural and commercial activity. A publisher, therefore, has to maintain a balance between the cultural and commercial demands of the publishing industry.

## STRUCTURE OF A PUBLISHING HOUSE

Publishing houses are indispensable intermediary points in the diffusion of ideas. If the market place of ideas is to allow the blooming of many flowers, it is of the essence that there exists a publishing industry, capable of fostering diverse intellectual and literary products that compete for attention of the public.

Publishing houses may be classified into big, small and modest The classification is guided by the number of titles, figure of sales, gross receipts, number of men employed to do various jobs and the number of departments looking after the publishing process. Whatever the size of a publisher, they perform more or less the same functions with difference in quantum.

Every publishing house, big or small, has the same inputs (Their number will determine the bigness or smallness of a publishing house) in the form of manuscripts and capital and produces an output (the book) for the market and readers. The overall structure of a publishing house may differ from the other, because of size of operations. Publishing work can be divided into the following four general areas:

1. *Editorial:* deals with acquisition of manuscript and its development.
2. *Production:* carries out the manufacturing or transforming the manuscript developed by the editorial section into a finished book.
3. *Sales and Promotion:* takes books to the readers through promotion, actual selling and merchandising.
4. *Administration:* concerns primarily with the management of administration and business of the publishing house by providing essential financial resources, administrative services and managing personnel and accounts.

A graphic representation of the structure of a publishing house would be as follows:

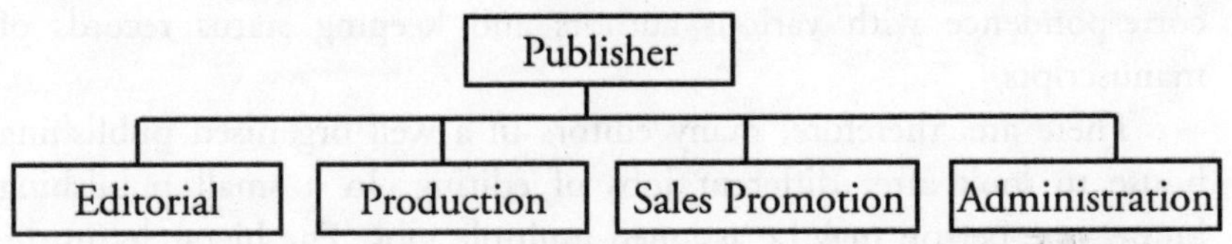


## EDITORIAL

The editorial department deals with the acquisition of manuscript and developing it to make it more readable and saleable. The task of the editorial department is, therefore, twofold; selection of manuscript and its preparation for publication. The success or failure of editorial department, even of publishing house, depends upon what has been recommended for publication, because most publishing failures are due to wrong editorial decisions.

What to publish and where to get it from is the basic principle of acquisition of manuscript. The manuscript may be solicited or unsolicited. The editor may conceive an idea and find an author to translate the idea into a written book or it may come to the editor's desk directly from the author, his agent, professional contact, through a friend or any other means, its merit and saleability is satisfied by the evaluation procedure before conveying yes or no to the author.

In the process of evaluation of a manuscript the editor works closely with other departments of the publishing house to get a feed back on the production cost and sale forecasts and to coordinate how best to produce and sell the book.

The editorial department carries the policy and programme of the publishing house by developing publisher's list according to the organisation's publishing philosophy. It is on these guidelines the authors and subjects are identified and approached, manuscripts developed and each title is promoted to the target audience.

The editorial department deals with the manuscript more closely and, therefore, remains in contact with the author more than any other department of the publishing house. In the process intimate relationship with the author is established which may sometimes result in further manuscripts by the author and his acquaintances.

The editorial department is also responsible for communication with the authors, checking, sorting and directing incoming manuscripts, returning rejected ones, maintaining files of correspondence with various authors and keeping status records of manuscripts.

There are, therefore, many editors in a well organised publishing house to look after different jobs of editing. In a small publishing house, one person may be assigned multiple jobs. The hierarchy in the editorial department may have a chief editor or managing editor at the helm. This is a supervisory position but in some cases, the chief editor may also look after the acquisition of manuscript and other related jobs. The main job of the chief editor is to coordinate and supervise the work of various editors working in the publishing house by keeping track of schedules and liaison with other departments of the publishing house.

There are sponsoring editors and desk editors who hunt for authors to write for the publishing house and attend to the unsolicited manuscripts which reach publishing house respectively.

The editorial department does the re-examination of the accepted manuscript by going through it, line by line, by improving the clarity and correctness of the manuscript and by specifically instructing the printer on matters concerning style, typeface and design. The process of going through the manuscript and making such changes is called copy-editing and the editor who does this job is known as copy-editor. In certain cases copyediting may involve a little more than a quick check for errors of fact, grammar and punctuation while in others, it may lead to major organisational and rewriting changes.

A large publishing house may also have a production editor, who is responsible for seeing a manuscript through printing and binding to finished publication, acting throughout the process of book production as liaison between the editorial department and production department. The house style where it exists is consistently followed. The complete copy-edited copy is passed on to the production section for transforming it into a book.

## PRODUCTION

Production department is responsible for the physical appearance and manufacturing of the book. Its job is to transform loosely written manuscript into a finished book by deciding the typesetting, printing and binding of the book. It also involves decision regarding the process of printing to be applied and the type of paper to be used and the kind of binding to be given to the book. It estimates the cost and decides how economically a given manuscript can be produced. The work involves computing production costs, and estimating break even figures, choosing services and materials and maintaining and controlling production budget.

The maxim that a good book must rest in a suitable body is the essence of the role of production department Very few people who read books realise that each book that is published is designed for ease and pleasure of reading.

Visualising a book and translating the concept into action by planning and specifying the visual attributes of the book, bearing in mind the theme and the thought of the author, is known as book designing. It also means to plan and specify all the graphic and physical elements of a publication.

Some publishing houses have their own designing department while most others depend upon free lance designers and with the introduction of Desk Top Publishing and computers the work can be taken care of by the phototypesetter or composer. But the need to have some person in the production department to look after this aspect so that the department can have an idea about how the book should look after publication can not be under estimated.

The design department or designer in a production department is required to take certain decisions about the physical appearance of each book. The production department would have some rough idea about the approximate length of the manuscript because of participation in the evaluation exercise of the editorial department. Balancing of the following factors is the key to successful book designing.

1. Suitability of design to the subject matter of the book
2. Attractiveness
3. Clarity and readability for the readers
4. Economy for the publisher as well as the purchaser
5. Feasibility for the printer

Production manager usually heads the production section in a publishing house. To justify his role the incumbent should have thorough knowledge of typography, printing and latest developments in these areas.

When a copy-edited manuscript is received by the production department for transforming into a book, information about the size of the edition, standard of production and approximate date by which the book should be ready, is also passed on. The process of converting the manuscript into a finished book involves certain decisions which are required to be taken by the production section. These include:

1. *Casting off:* Estimating number of pages that a particular manuscript will take when typeset is called casting off. A page estimate is arrived at by making a character or word count of the whole manuscript and dividing that by the number of words anticipated on each type set page, within a given typeface, design and print area.

A more precise analysis is derived from a *break down,* which is count of the various types of materials such as text, tables, footnotes etc. The idea is to arrive at an estimated number of printed pages the manuscript will occupy when set and made up. Printers' copy-fitting tables can assist in arriving at the estimated figure.

The casting off exercise would also enable the production department to work out the near exact cost of production. Though a rough estimate of the cost of production would have already been worked out at the time of evaluation of manuscript, the details of the cost involved in each operation would give nearly exact idea of the cost of production of a book.

2. *Designing the text*: This includes decision about the typeface, type size and the print area. This would be guided by the subject matter of the book and readers for whom the book is intended. A large variety of type faces is available. Each typeface has its own characteristics. Readability and legibility are the two fundamental characteristics which one should never forget while deciding the typeface. Readability is the characteristic of the body of type that makes it comfortable to read. Legibility, on the other hand is the quality of type that makes it possible to read. Legibility depends upon the white space within a letter and between letters. Readability is also contributed by the size of the typeface, length of the line and spacing between words, lines and margins. Colour and texture of the paper should be in relationship with the subject matter of the book.

Margins are important, therefore, should be as generous as possible consistent with the length of the print matter and within the cost consideration. More margin would mean lesser number of words per page and more pages for completing the text. Nevertheless, margins contribute towards reading comfort.

3. *Parts of the book and preliminary pages:* Text pages, appendix and index constitute parts of the book. It is not essential that each book should have all the three parts. But for proper estimate of the length of the book decision is taken regarding preliminary pages and other parts of the book.

Preliminary pages also known as front matter run in the following sequence:

(i) half title, (ii) back of the half title page, (iii) title page, (iv) copyright page, (v) dedication, (vi) acknowledgement, (vii) preface, (viii) Contents. Information about appendix and index to be included should also be counted and planned for.

Some books may have all or some of the preliminary pages. Others may or may not have appendix or index. There is no fixed rule for the arrangement of type on the preliminary pages, but through judicious selection, sense of logic and balance, the designer may select the size and kind of type which will be in harmony with the main text of the book.

4. *Selection of paper:* Selection of paper for text of a book is a major decision because paper cost goes up and down directly in proportion to the size of the edition. Factors that influence the selection of paper would include weight, strength, opacity, surface texture, colour and its folding quality. Absorption of ink and resistance to moisture are other considerations which a production manager would look for while deciding the paper for the text.

Production manager, therefore, should have thorough knowledge of the characteristics of the kinds of paper available in the market within the permissible budget. Cost of paper, though not a characteristic, is a basic factor in decision making. Any faultering in this will take the price of the book on the higher side which may look unaffordable by the readers.

Subject matter of thc book and the intended readership also play a vital role in selecting the paper. For example: weight of paper needed for children books is much more than a college text book. Suitability to printing process is also a key factor. In fact, the choice of paper and choice of process of printing are interdependent.

5. *Selection of process of printing:* Books are generally printed on one of the three basic processes of printing: Letterpress, Offset and Gravure.

Letterpress is a traditional process in which images are transferred by pressure from an inked raised relief plate to the material being printed through the operation of a machine.

Offset printing, on the other hand, causes ink to be transferred first to a blanket surface and then to paper from a plate on which the printing and non printing areas are on the same level, but the non printing areas are wetted so that they will not print while the printing areas are quoted with a greasy ink that resist the water.

Gravure (also known as intaglio) is printing from a plate into which an image has been cut rather than raised, as in relief printing (letter press). As the image has been cut below the surface of the plate, when the plate is inked, the ink flows into the cuts, then when excess ink is cleared off the surface of the plate, the ink remaining in the cuts, prints on paper in contact with the plate.

The processes briefly mentioned above have their advantages and disadvantages. Those have been discussed in detail in later chapters. Production manager's decision will be guided by suitability of the process, number of copies to be printed, the ability and capacity of the printer to deliver the desired quality within the provided time frame.

6. *Binding of the book:* If we go back to the definition of a book, it is the element of binding which distinguishes book from loosely kept sheets of printed materials. The process of, binding involves folding of large printed sheets down to book size, gathering the folded sheets in a continuous sequence sewing or fastening them together and attaching the end paper and covering them.

Many options are available, depending upon the nature of the book: the selling price which the publisher wants to keep and the money which he can afford for the binding of the book. The book can be case bound (hard bound), paper bound, staple stitched or spiral bound. School books can be sewn and paper bound. Reference books can be hard bound. A similar decision is expected from the production manager which will be in line with the overall production of the book.

7. *Selection of services:* There are only a few publishing houses which have inhouse production facilities. Most others have to depend upon outside suppliers and services for designing, printing and binding of books. It is, therefore, essential that a complete control of the time schedule is kept by the production department. Instructions to service and material suppliers should be complete and unambiguous to achieve the final product at lowered cost with improved quality.

Speed is the pass word of the production department. Tight schedules, daily pressures, insistence of editorial department to rush through a publication to meet some deadline date, pose tremendous challenges to the job of production manager. Diplomatic with colleagues within the publishing house and suppliers outside the publishing house require great deal of patience with firmness to get the work done in time.

A good production manager should be able to handle short term or long term pressures while keeping one's cool, be highly organised, have considerable foresight and meticulous worker who can attend to every detail. Efficiency and economy is what one looks for into a production manager.

The process of manufacturing the book may complete with the role of production department. The process of publishing does not end there. The process completes only when a book reaches the hands of the readers and this job is performed by the Sales promotion department.

## SALES PROMOTION

Sales promotion department's association with the book begins at its conceptual stage when editorial department consults the sales promotion section to find out the sale possibilities at the time of accepting the manuscript. The real responsibility falls upon the department when a finished book is passed on to the publisher's warehouse by the production department.

A thoughtfully selected, skillfully edited and creatively produced book will be of no use to its publisher if it fails to reach the intended purchasers. The main job of the sales promotion department, therefore, is to let the people know about the publication of the book and make them want to buy it.

Sales promotion department in a medium size publishing house will consist of a sales promotion manager, area sales representatives. The Sales manager communicates and explains the publishing house's policy on matters of discounts and other incentives to the sales staff. He is responsible for preparing and implementing the sales promotion plan (discussed separately in later chapter), allotting sales quotas to sales staff and reviewing and revising the plan according to the circumstances. For successful working of the sales promotion plan, the sales manager also communicates directly with the trade channels and customers.

This department plays a very vital role in the publishing cycle. It brings money back to the publishing house. To fulfill this main objective sales promotion department performs variety of functions which may be divided into two categories:

Sales Function

Promotion Function

*Sales Function:* By selling books, the department not only brings money back to the publishing house but also takes books to the ultimate readers for whom it had been printed. The challenging job of selling requires:

1. Identifying the market
2. Choosing the sales channels
3. Actual selling

Publisher's market consists of four major customers (i) Wholesalers (ii) Retailers (iii) Institutions and Organisations (iv) Individual buyers. Majority of sale orders come from wholesalers who in turn sell to their nearest retailers. Retailers further look after the institutions and individual buyers. The system works like this. The wholesaler buys books directly from the publisher at a certain discount, which these days goes up to 50% of the published price and sells them to the retailers at 25% to 40% depending upon the number of copies ordered by the retailer and nature of publication. Retailer further sells books to the institutions and individual buyers at 10 to 15% discount, thereby retaining a certain percentage of discount.

Sales department also compiles a list of wholesalers and retailers. These trade channels are sometimes categorised according to nature of their merchandise *i.e.* general bookseller, wholesaler or retailer of scientific and technical books etc., so that the sales promotion material is well targetted.

To fulfil the selling function, sales representatives visit wholesalers, retailers and libraries regularly, keeping them informed about the new arrivals, trade terms and deliver publicity materials which the sales promotion department has prepared for promoting new and old titles. The number of sales representatives in a publishing house will depend upon the annual turnover and number of new titles published by a publishing house.

The sales representatives serve as a link between the publisher and the market and provide useful feedback on the success or lack of, promotion plan which is sometime altered on the advice of the sales staff.

Each sales representative is allotted an area or region who in turn works under a sales manager who usually looks after national sales and is responsible for preparation of materials that the sales representatives need and carry with them when they visit the allotted market.

Sales representatives provide necessary feedback on the reaction of the market to book prices, discounts, return policy and such other matters which help in adjusting the sales promotion plan.

The sales department is also responsible for direct selling, developing display materials to be used in sales promotion. The department may arrange for special sales by arranging premium sales at fairs, conferences and special meetings of organisations including participation in sale of subsidiary rights of the book.

*Promotion Function*: Sales functions can not be performed in isolation. Sales is an integral part of the promotion function of the sales promotion department of a publishing house. Promotion is a marketing activity. It includes all efforts made by the publisher to inform the potential readers about the existence of the book and prompting them to buy it.

Promotional activities would include publicity, generating interest in the book through the use of print media, radio, television, through book reviews, seminars and discussions, including lecture tours and autograph sessions by the author.

Advertising, with the help of inhouse staff or outside agencies, if the budget permits, is also done to promote books. Book advertisement is a costly affair. Only a book with major potential can receive advertisement exposure. Advertisement, however, is a key tool for direct selling by obtaining direct orders from consumers.

Other promotional methods include preparation of catalogues, supplying posters and other display materials and participation in book exhibitions.

Getting books reviewed in newspapers and magazines provide free publicity and advertising. Promotion manager sends review copies to review media and follows up with the newspaper and magazine editors.

Book promotion starts before a book is published and continues ever after the book is sold so that the publishing house's name is kept in public eye.

It is sales promotion department which fulfils the dream of a publisher to run the business in profit by adopting ways and means by which a book is sold to bring in certain profits for the publishing house (detailed discussion on Sales Promotion follows in later chapter).

Editorial, production and sales, though responsible for individual areas of book publishing, there is administration and accounts section which coordinates and controls the three departments.

## ADMINISTRATION AND ACCOUNTS

This is the coordinating and controlling department which is associated with every stage of publishing process; though not participating technically in the selection of manuscript, physical manufacture and promotion of the book, yet by allocating the funds for each of the operation involved in book production. This is the department which controls the finance. Usually the publisher himself heads this department or by deputing somebody who works under him and reports directly to him.

The department provides at any given point of time, financial information which is very essential to run and control a business. It also does cost analysis of various operations in book publishing, provides guidelines where expenditure needs to be cut and where money is available for utilisation. The department combines the dual responsibility of doing business and running the administration of the publishing house.

Main functions of the department are:

1. The processing of orders, receipts from wholesalers and retailers etc. and payments to suppliers of materials and services.
2. Recruitment and management of personnel, deciding salaries and terms of payments, deciding promotion procedures and arranging part time services and in house training.
3. Purchase of materials on behalf of other departments and supply of stationery to each department, for day to day functioning.
4. Keeps the company accounts up to date so that at any given point of time a statement of financial standing of the company is made available for its own knowledge and for comparing company's performance in relation to other publishing houses.
5. All official assistance regarding filing and maintenance of records etc. is provided by this section.

These and many more, depending upon the needs and size of an individual publishing house, are the functions of a well organised publishing house. For the success of a publishing house each department, though has independent field of activity, has to work in unison and as a team.

In the foregoing paragraphs, a brief picture of the structure of a publishing house has been drawn. A detailed narrative of editorial, production and sales promotion is given in the following chapters.

# Part II

## Editorial Department—Creating the Book

# 3

# Acquisition of Manuscript

Flow of manuscripts into a publishing house is the life blood which is very vital for the growth and development of the company. Search of manuscripts and initiating projects that will result into books and meet the needs of the publishing house, is the responsibility for the editorial department. Its job is to seek out, buy and edit books that the company would like to publish. Building up of a saleable list is the essence of successful publishing.

In the words of Datus C. Smith "The publisher who sits waiting for authors and translators to bring in manuscripts is going to publish an undistinguished list of books—and have small profit. On the other hand, the publisher who wants to give good service both to the public interest and to its firm's profit goes out and gets manuscripts."

There are many ways by which a book project can be developed into a book. The idea can come to the editor from within the publishing house or out side it. Editors search for writing talent, whenever they find it, they get in touch with the promising new writers. The editors must keep an open door to all who come to them with new ideas. These book ideas may come from many places. Some of the sources identified by publishers from where manuscripts and book proposals come to editors are enumerated below.

## SOURCES OF MANUSCRIPTS

1. Ideas from within the publishing house.
2. Discovery of book idea/author by reading/attending conferences.
3. Commissioning of a manuscript.
4. Literary scouts.
5. Literary agents.
6. Unsolicited manuscripts.

1. *Ideas from Within the Publishing House*

The acquisition of publishable manuscripts is the sole responsibility of the editorial department. But the idea can originate from any other functionary of the publishing house. People working in production and sales department are also fully conversant with the publishing programme of the company. They are aware of the area of experimentation and field of activity of the publishing house. These men come in contact with professors, librarians, book reviewers and authors in the process of their work of producing and promoting the books. In the process they may come to know of a prospective writer who has either written or can write the kind of books needed by the publishing house or the type of ideas the editors are on the look out. These prospective authors are introduced to the editors of the publishing house who welcome such suggestions and sometime may succeed in finalising a proposal.

2. *Discovery of Author or Book Idea by Reading/Attending Conferences*

An ideal editor is said to be a superman, with world of events as well as literatures at his fingertips. "Editors read widely and with catholicity of taste. They must, if they are to keep their jobs. Else they will be taken over by their competitors." The editor of school or college text book acquires knowledge of the educational system by being part of the system or by studying and reading about it. Editors read other publishers, catalogues to find out what is new in the market. What competition the new manuscript will have to face. They follow not only creative writing but also critical writing, watch closely the publications of their own trade, attend conferences/seminars to contact established authors and explore possibilities of the potential authors and manuscripts.

3. *Commissioning of Manuscript*

Publishers directly influence the content of what is written. The most pervasive and direct way the publisher can influence this is to conceive of a work and commission an author to write it. The essence of successful publishing is 'what to publish' and 'where to get it from.' The publishers must be aware of what authors are writing and what readers want and need. When works for which potential market exists, are not being produced, the publishers may commission them. This probably occurs most frequently where publishing is highly developed; but it can be specially important where traditions of authorship are not firmly established.

It appears to be increasingly common for works to have their genesis in publisher's rather than author's mind. Publishers call themselves 'shapers of culture' and 'gatekeepers of ideas.' They operate as sluice gates, they are gatekeepers in as much as they are empowered to make decision on what to let 'in' and what to keep 'out'. They function as arbiters of taste and culture. There is considerable interaction between editors and authors and this interaction often shapes the nature of what is published.

4. *Literary Scouts*

A direct personal recommendation to an editor is a common way for an author to be introduced to an editor for possible publication of a manuscript. Editors sometimes depend upon outsiders, generally a university professor, teacher, librarian, bookseller or scholar to keep watch on what is being written in their respective specialised fields. This is both common and important manner of acquiring manuscripts.

A literary scout is one who researches for publishable literary property on behalf of a publishing house and is usually compensated by the publisher if a recommended property such as book idea of a manuscript is contracted.

A large number of scholarly and university level text books are received by this way. Some scouts work for more than one publisher and often become responsible for authors leaving publishers. They do not exist in large number but, nevertheless, are important source of acquisition of manuscripts by publishing houses.

5. *Literary Agents*

Another way an editor hears about a publishing proposal is through literary agent. These agents are the most recognised sources of such communication. In England and America, literary agents have become an important factor in publishing. 'An author who does not employ agent these days is rare, and the publisher who does not advise an author to use agent is even rarer.' The institution of literary agents have taken solid roots in the West, it is not as important a factor in India, though there are some operating in the Indian publishing arena.

Literary agents are men or women, who either alone or as members of firms, place the manuscripts of their client authors with publishers. Because, they know what the publishers are buying and who is publishing what. They have an intimate knowledge of the lists of various publishing houses.

Literary agents receive commission, usually 10 per cent but sometime 15 per cent-of all receipts and they negotiate the terms of publishing contract on behalf of authors.

They are twentieth century phenomenon whose business depend upon personal contact, on the ability to attract author customers to themselves and to sell their wares to publishing trade, film makers and broadcasters.

Initially, publishers resisted the advent of literary agents as middlemen between authors and publishers and who could disturb the 'cosy intimacy' between them. The hostility has now become less pronounced when publishers realised they intend to do a wonderful job of screening material and stopping such bad manuscripts from reaching the editor's desk by submitting only what appears to have some kind of reasonable chance of acceptance.

The literary agent's role is immensely complex and played on many different levels. They are a link between the author and his publisher and a literary agent must satisfy both equally.

They have three basic functions:

*Editorial:* They help authors define and refine their own ideas and revise manuscripts after submission.

*Placing:* Literary agents try to fix the most suitable publisher and try to sell subsidiary rights at profitable terms.

*Selling:* By trying to get best possible terms for the author while signing the contract.

They sometimes perform 'such disparate services as midwife, middlemen and auctioneers,' says Thomas Weyr. 'As midwives they are often instrumental in delivering a book from the author and later to the publisher. As middlemen, they negotiate with editors for sale of books, and they auction books if the property can be best handled in a bidding situation.'

Though literary agents are totally identified with the authors, their relationship with publishers and their editors is friendly. They often have to educate authors in publishing problems. A middleman's dialogue goes both ways. You can not force a book down a publisher's throat.

Good agents, who have highly developed ability to evaluate all forms of literary propositions can earn for their authors sums which the authors could seldom expect to obtain for themselves.

### 6. *Unsolicited Manuscripts*

A large number of manuscripts are received by publishing houses unsolicited, also called 'over the transom.' These are called unsolicited because they arrive at publisher's office at author's own initiative and unexpectedly and without being asked by the publishing house to do so. These manuscripts are neither commissioned by publishers nor recommended by their editors.

Such submissions outnumber any other way of submission of manuscript and, therefore, warrants detailed information. To an author, sending a manuscript or an idea to a publisher may seem so logical way of attracting attention. But unfortunately, publishers receive so many of them that they can not give them sufficient attention.

Though no exact figures regarding unsolicited manuscripts submitted in every year are available in India or elsewhere, yet the fact remains that staggering number keeps on pouring everyday.

It may seem astonishing why there are so many unsolicited manuscripts and why only a few of them see the light of the day. The reason is not far to seek. Although, authors may do a lot of labour on writing the manuscript, they do little research in finding out who would be interested in that kind of manuscript.

Another reason for mass rejection of unsolicited manuscripts is that—many unknown beginners try to start with the largest and most prestigious publishing houses. Finally the numbers of unsolicited manuscripts are swelled by the simple fact that many authors indulge in multiple submission and send copies of the manuscripts to large number of publishing houses simultaneously.

Some publishers reject manuscripts with great speed. For most publishers the standard reason for turning down an unsolicited manuscript is 'it does not fall within our list.' There are other reasons too. Few authors would realise that each manuscript received by publishers whether rejected, as the majority are bound to be or accepted, costs the publisher some money. Publishers are choosy and they have to, because they know that most authors are known failures and they make their living out of a few successes.

The general accusation that publishers reject manuscript without reading can not be accepted wholly. Because it is rare that a publisher will refuse to consider a manuscript that sounds at all possible.

The views expressed by Narendra Kumar on this aspect are symbolic of what most publishers feel. He said "Publishers can not afford to spend time on reading a manuscript beyond the point at which one gets convinced that it has no chance of acceptance; no purpose would be served by such pointless reading; It will only delay conveying decision of the publisher. How much a manuscript is read could vary from a few pages, through a few chapters, to a whole work." Most authors also forget Dr. Samuel Johnson's remarks that "it is unnecessary to eat the whole ox to find out whether the beef is tough."

The point that publishers as a class are not interested in works of new authors is not to be accepted without reservation. Unrequested manuscripts pour in all the time even though, a few pompous publishers actually refuse to accept work that has not been invited or commissioned. But if everybody 'adopted this prissy attitude, there would have been no *Gone with the Wind,* the classic example of a best seller that literally came to its publisher through post'.

# 4

# Recording the Incoming Manuscript

The moment a manuscript arrives at editor's desk, no matter from what source, the work of handling the incoming manuscripts is set in motion. A good editor should be a good housekeeper. The editor should maintain a proper record of receiving and controlling the incoming manuscripts by following some system of entering them that would facilitate the follow up work on the manuscripts. This is advised not only for convenience of keeping records, it is also necessary for healthy public relations with authors. Editors should always remember that no publishing whatsoever is possible without manuscripts and for providing manuscripts, there must be authors whose nurture and goodwill is the chief concern in publishing.

For achieving this, prior to decision making, the manuscript should be immediately entered into some record file and acknowledged. Though keeping record and follow up of each incoming manuscript is a costly affair editors will do well to still maintain these records and save the publishing house from any further embarrassment from the author which may be caused if the manuscript is either lost or misplaced in the publishing house. The possibility of such happenings are many if such track is not maintained.

The following steps are usually taken to handle the incoming manuscript:

1. The manuscript should be immediately acknowledged explaining to the author that though every care will be taken of the manuscript, the publishing house will not be responsible for any loss or damage. This is possible because of large number of unsolicited manuscripts that keep on pouring in at editor's desk everyday. This does not mean that one should become careless, but by doing so, the author has been cautioned for any such eventuality.

2. On a checklist or card/file the date of receipt and the name and address of the sender should be entered.
3. Editor should note down author's instructions, if any, about the return of the manuscript.
4. The names of the inhouse reader and expert, outside reader with date should be mentioned on the record sheet so that at any given point of time it may be possible to locate the manuscript. This is important because in the mad rush of editorial work for a large number of books, the editor can forget as to whom the manuscript has been sent for reading and comments.
5. On the return of the manuscript from the reader, the date of return should also be mentioned.
6. A note whether any illustrations, tables or any auxiliary material has been sent alongwith the manuscript be made.
7. List of incoming manuscripts should be circulated among the other editorial staff so that others connected with the job may also keep a track of the movement of the manuscript.
8. Any other information which is relevant to the manuscript should also be mentioned on the record sheet.

It is a matter of common knowledge that not all manuscripts produced by the authors are published. It is the prerogative of the publisher to decide which manuscript should be accepted for publication and which should be rejected.

For all publishers, the decision to accept or reject a manuscript is also an economic decision. It takes us to a point where an editor is to play a strategic role in the process of editorial development by applying his qualities of head and heart in opting for books which will sell, because, all publishing failures are due to wrong editorial decisions. It is also said that if an editor thinks right for the posterity, he thinks wrong for the balance sheet. "Few things delight the heart of a publisher," writes Mark Goulden, "more than the discovery of a new writing talent. It does not happen very often. Some publishers have never even made a notable discovery."

It is only through sound judgement that an editor can make an enduring success of publishing. The procedure for evaluating proposals and manuscripts, though not consistent and common in various publishing houses, is of fundamental importance.

# 5

# Evaluation of Manuscript

The discussion in the previous chapter provides us a glimpse of various ways by which a manuscript can come to a publishing house for consideration. It is the responsibility of the editorial department to hunt for publishable and saleable manuscripts. Other departments also, in some way or the other, are involved in the process of decision making. No matter through which route the proposal has landed at the editor's desk, the next important work in the process of book publishing is evaluation of manuscript or deciding whether or not the submitted manuscript is suitable for publication.

## EVALUATION DEFINED

Evaluation of manuscript can be defined as selection of manuscript for publication on the basis of marketability, price and need for it. Evaluation of manuscript is also known as macro editing in which the editor assesses the publishable qualities of the manuscript. It is the study and examination of the manuscript to find out:

1. whether it contains anything of intrinsic merit which can be converted into a book;
2. whether the submitted manuscript suits the publisher's list;
3. whether the product is easily marketable; and
4. whether it can be produced at a price which is affordable.

Evaluation of manuscript also known as vetting of manuscript can be defined as the 'checking and examining the newly born baby in order to see that he is sound, healthy and physically strong to carry on a normal healthy life and is not bounded by medical aids every now and then.'

Whenever an editor looks at a manuscript, decides to go on reading, or on the other hand, puts manuscript down, thinks whether or not this is the kind of book needed or tries to consider the acceptability in the market, he is making some kind of judgement. As he goes on reading the pages and thinks that the work is very good, very bad or just indifferent or that it is not merely good but potentially great, he is making judgement over the manuscript at hand. He is unconsciously evaluating the manuscript.

## NEED FOR EVALUATION

There are so many unsolicited manuscripts received by publishers and so few of them are finally accepted for publication. It is crucial to the dissemination of knowledge that all manuscripts submitted should not be accepted. "There are two reasons why a publisher publishes a book," said Prof. V.V. John "One is its commercial value and if he has to stay in business he has to consider that first, second being the prestige."

For all publishers decision to accept or reject a manuscript is in part an economic decision. This is true for commercial and non-profit publisher alike. Commercial publisher has to earn profit—non commercial publisher has to avoid loosing his capital. Few authors realise that on an average each manuscript received by a publisher whether rejected or accepted, costs the publisher some money. But despite this fact, it is rare that a publisher will refuse to consider a manuscript that sounds at all possible.

Publishers may say that every manuscript is faithfully read, but that may not be always true. Publishers can not afford to spend time on reading a manuscript beyond a point at which the editor gets convinced that it has no chance of acceptance. No purpose would be served by such pointless reading. How much a manuscript is read could vary from a few pages, through a few chapters, to a whole book.

Publishers are choosy and they have to be because they know that most authors are known to be failures. They make their living out of a few successes and if they are 'indulgent with less successful authors, they can not hope to make an enduring success of publishing.'

## EVALUATION PROCEDURE

The procedure for reviewing, evaluating and deciding to publish, differs considerably from house to house. In some publishing houses, the job is left to the editor alone, while in others, the matter is discussed in the editorial meetings when other top functionaries of the publishing house also participate and take a collective decision and aspects of suitability, marketability, price, cost of production, size of the edition etc., are deliberated. Sometimes, views of sales and production department are invited separately to help the decision making process.

Discussed below is the typical procedure followed by an average well organised publishing house.

*Suitability of Manuscript:* Even though salability is the basic factor to be considered, there are other factors which are taken into consideration even before the salability. Before thinking of salability of manuscript, editor will have to see the suitability of the manuscript to the publishing programme of the publishing house. Does it fall within the list? Editor would ask to himself.

Some manuscripts are outrightly rejected because either they are very poorly written or they are unsuitable for that publishing house. For example, a book on cooking, or even a fiction would be unsuitable for a publisher of religious books. Similarly a scholarly book on religion may not be accepted by a publisher of children literature. Therefore, suitability before salability is what the editor looks for in a manuscript.

The easiest thing in a publishing house is to reject a manuscript. The reward of publishing, intellectual and otherwise lies in deciding on the books on which a publisher may perhaps says 'yes' or 'may be'. Assuming that the manuscript falls within the list and it appears to have sale potential the editor has to look at the manuscript more seriously.

*In House Reading:* This is done by some one in the editorial staff for 'sampling and overview'. In a small publishing house the job of reading the manuscript (also called first reading) is done by the editor. The manuscript, is read from the point of view of general competence.

The first reader will prepare a short note on the quality of the manuscript, the effect it is going to have on the readers, the originality of ideas, coherence and presentation of the arguments.

If the manuscript is lacking in these, it will be rejected without further consideration. If it shows some promise, further investigation on the possibility of the manuscript will be made.

*Effect:* While going through the manuscript, the editor would like to assess the effect it is going to have on readers. If it is an instructional book, has the author succeeded in making the concepts clear or has further confused the readers? If the author has set out to entertain, does the. author succeed in that? If the book is not a reading experience, neither the editor nor the ultimate reader can read it with interest. If it is a mystery, can it provide breathless attention? What the editor is looking for in a publishable manuscript, besides many other things, is the desired effect of clear, direct and graceful presentation.

*Presentation:* Some people believe that except for creative literature, style of writing in a book is obviously less important than the contents. Nevertheless, readers often enjoy even a factual book if it has a better manner of presentation of facts. The arrangement of material, therefore, assumes greater significance. Though author has a choice among several acceptable patterns, like chronological, logical, developmental and a few others, the choice should depend upon the subject matter and the readership for whom the book is being prepared. Coherence in the presentation of material facilitates understanding of the subject and provides quick access to specific bits of information.

*Coherence:* The whole manuscript should be well knit, logically developed in which subject matter is coherently arranged. There should not be meaningless pouring of words and sentences. The writing should be precise and concise. The points of explanation should not have been dragged much too long for its importance. The author should have avoided ineffective looseness which invariably creeps in if the manuscript lacks in originality.

*Originality:* It is very difficult task to tell what originality means when it comes to writing by authors and its evaluation by editors. As one author has put it 'Every author lives on the shoulders of his predecessor.' But what editor would be looking for is something entirely fresh and novel and not derivative, flat or completely uninspiring and unoriginal. It is only the originality of presentation which can make the writing look hackneyed or bright. The idea may be age old.

*Outside Expert Reader:* If the manuscript is on a subject on which the first reader (in house reader) does not have specialised knowledge, but the manuscript is showing some promise, the same is referred to an outside reader also called expert reader. The outside reader or reviewer is usually a specialist in the subject or an authority on literary style. University teachers, professors and authors who have already written or worked in the subject area are chosen as expert readers. The use of expert reader in the evaluation process is very common in university level texts and scholarly books. These experts go through the manuscripts and advise the publishers about the merits of the book. They are paid some reading fee by the publisher.

Keeping in view the cost involved some publishers hesitate to refer the manuscript to expert readers which is a bad economics. The money saved as reading fee is nothing compared to possible loss which the publisher may incur by accepting a manuscript which should have been declined. On the other hand publisher's editor should have strong sense of discrimination in deciding which manuscript should be sent for outside review. One can not go on spending reading fee on books on which one finally has to say no.

If the suggestions by the outside reader can help the publisher in decision making, it can also prejudice the decision if the outside reader is not objective in his recommendations. Certain precautions, therefore, are necessary in appointing an outside expert.

*Choice:* Outside reader should be knowledgeable person with a sense of high objectivity.

*Reliability:* The expert should be reliable person in the sense that the publisher could depend upon his recommendations. His assessment should be based on thorough study of the manuscript.

*Impartiality:* The outside reader should be able to forward his opinion about the manuscript without any bias for or against the subject or the author.

*Anonymity:* Complete anonymity should be maintained about the name of the author and the name of the outside reader. Neither the author nor the reader should know each other's identity at least until the editor has decided to consider the manuscript for publication. Because if the anonymity is broken, the recommendations can be influenced to the disadvantage of the publisher.

The expert reader may be asked to give an opinion on areas like correctness of the matter, uptodateness and such other areas which may help the editor in the decision making process.

## INVESTIGATION OF COMPETITION

Competition is a symbol of affluence, abundance and good health. The sense of competition is born in man's urge for betterment of life and style. The total effect of competition is dynamism. A situation in human life without competition faces stagnation and vacuum.

The urge for bringing out better books by publishers bring in the competition in the realm of book publishing. The first person saddled with the responsibility of investigation of competition is the editor. As soon as an idea occurs to him or an editor gets a manuscript for consideration, he applies the criteria of competition and compares the manuscript with the list of the publishing house. The competition has to be measured from within and outside the publishing house. The following factors are borne in mind:

1. If a book on the same subject is already on the publisher's list, is it worthwhile to consider another title on the same subject?
2. Whether the book already on the list is selling well?
3. Will the present manuscript be really able to stand up in competition from comparable books by other publishers?
4. Does the offered manuscript register some improvement over the earlier published books?
5. Will it cover more efficiently the particular requirements of a course or a subject than the earlier books?

## EXAMINATION OF COMPETITION

The editors are widely read people. They are supposed to have an intimate knowledge of the field of activity of the publishing house. They should also have a watch over what other publishers are doing in the same area of activity.

The editor would examine the competition for the new manuscript keeping in mind the following areas.

1. *Coverage:* The coverage of the proposed book is going to have a great bearing on the decision making process. What are the contents of the manuscript? Are they going to be of additional use to the readers? Will it interest them? Does this manuscript contain some new worthwhile information which may make the manuscript stand out in distinction? From the coverage angle each book falls under one of the three categories.

(1) Either the book has little than needed, (2) or it has more than needed, (3) or it has just that is needed. To which category the manuscript in hand belongs will give an idea about the coverage.

2. *Updateness:* An important factor in measuring the competition and which also helps in the decision making is updateness of the manuscript. Editor would see whether the material is recent enough to provide uptodate information on a given subject. Publishers usually stress upon the recency of the book so that readers would be impressed that the book contains latest information. People seem to favour something new and innovative and, therefore, publishers publish latest or new edition of earlier published books. For example a book on history of banking in India after independence would have no updateness if it does not cover the bank nationalisation and after. Readers are definitely going to reject the book when they come to know that it is not uptodate on the subject.

3. *Author's Reputation (Authority):* Author's own bona fides are the best proof of the merits of a manuscript. What is the reputation of the author (as a writer)? What does he do? What is his status or position? What influence does he exercise in the field in which he is writing? What has been the success story or otherwise of his earlier published works? Whether the author is competent enough to write a book on the subject? These and many more questions are kept in mind by the editor while going through the process of evaluation. If information about the author is lacking, the editor may write back asking the author to send the detailed information. This piece of information called 'Author's Questionnaire' will provide answers to all such queries mentioned above. The information can subsequently be used in the book promotion, if the manuscript is accepted for publication.

4. *Publislters' Reputation:* The editor keeps a track of what other publishers are doing in a given area. Some publishers over the years have built up sound reputation for quality books in one or more fields. The manuscript in hand may have to stand in competition with the established, well reputed publishers. Though this factor should not discourage a publisher or his editor going ahead with a manuscript that has all the potentiality to take on any name.

5. *Production Cost:* Every editorial decision is also a financial decision. Though editor's criteria is largely academic, the financial aspect of book production can not loose sight. The cost of production has a direct bearing on the selling price and the selling price of a book has to be fixed keeping in view the nature of the manuscript and the

profile of the readers. Competition in terms of selling price of books published by other publishers on the same subject for the same kind of readers has to be taken into account. Sometimes, where compromise with the quality of production or reduction in the length of manuscript is not possible, the manuscript may have to be declined on this account only.

6. *Special Features:* The editor has to watch out for any additional feature which the author has provided to enhance the acceptability and salability of the book. The additional information in the form of appendix, bibliography, notes on books and references, useful tables and graphs may enhance the value of the book and can make the manuscript stand out in competition with other comparable books. These special features add to the reference value of the book and make it more acceptable to readers and libraries.

## CONSULTATION WITH SALES DEPARTMENT

The decision to publish may be good editorially but may make a bad business sense. The book may look excellent in its intellectual or literary aspect, but if the editor over estimates the sales or underestimates the cost, he may be heading for trouble. Before decision to publish a book has been taken, the editor would like to take advantage of the expert opinion of the sales and production department.

The information about manuscript, its subject, author etc., is passed on to the sales department to find out how many copies of that kind of book can be sold in the first, second and third year. The sales department with its experience in selling will provide estimates about the sale potential of the book, subsidiary rights possibilities, reprint and other projections. The editor would like the sales department to enlighten him on the following points:

1. Does this kind of a book have ready market?
2. If yes, how big is the market?
3. Has the subject been sold well in the past?
4. How many copies can be sold and how soon?
5. What is going to be likely life of the book in terms of years?
6. What should be the likely selling price? (This will, however, be worked out on the basis of cost estimates supplied by the production department.)

## CONSULTATION WITH PRODUCTION DEPARTMENT

The editor seeks the advise of the production department on vital points which play a significant role in the decision making process. The production department will comment upon the approximate length of the book as well as size of the first print run. It would provide break-Ups of various production costs and work out the unit cost of production. This will enable the editor to fix the estimated selling price and the possible break even. The department will also provide information about the time required for production of the book and also alternative methods of production to economise on costs.

The considerations editor keeps in mind while going through the evaluation process can be enumerated as under:

1. Does the manuscript fall within the list?
2. Will it sell?
3. Is it well written and contains something of value to the potential reader?
4. Does it have the commercial viability for exploitation of subsidiary and other rights?
5. Does it confirm to the accepted standard of good taste and decency?
6. Whether the manuscript is capable of being produced at the cost which will allow the retail price to be competitive?
7. Does it have an audience large enough to sustain its publication on economic basis?

## FINAL DECISION

The complexity of the problem of evaluation has been aptly described by Samuel Israel: He says, "The calculus is much more complex. None of the variables act in isolation. A lower price need not always lead to higher sales. High quality will not sell at any price. There is no absolute relation between the physical dimension/or physical quality of the book and price that will be considered right for it. A 600 page text book may well sell at the same price, as a 300 page autobiography with no complaint from the purchaser of the latter. A good book on a particular subject may not sell because there have been many books on the same subject coming out in rapid succession. On the other hand, a book that is not really excellent may well command spectacular sales if it comes at the right moment when the subject is hot and when nothing else is available."

Even after all the checks by the publishing staff and outsiders, the publishing decision may still be awaiting its final judgement. The criteria for financial success, as well as the methods through which this success is realised, differ considerably from one house to another; but the principle remains that publishing is above all a business and in a publishing house, it is the publisher who is the businessman.

The editor, no doubt, is the most important person in a publishing house, next only to the publisher, but he is not the publisher himself. The final nod of decision making, therefore, rests with the publisher. The editor will pass on the information about the manuscript gathered on the bases of various steps discussed above, to the publisher. The information is usually sent in the form of a note, detailing results of various consultations alongwith the editor's own assessment of the manuscript and recommendation.

With the information supplied, coupled with his own horse sense, personal knowledge and hunch, the publisher will take a decision about the manuscript. He will convey his approval for going ahead with the publication of the manuscript. If the publisher's decision is 'yes', the editor deals with the manuscript again. This time with a different job—copy editing the manuscript and preparing it for the press.

Before the editor or copy editor uses his pen or pencil on the manuscript for the purpose of copy editing, the copy editor has to satisfy himself that all parts of the book have been supplied by the author and that the manuscript is complete in all respects. A decision needs to be taken in consultation with the author about the parts of the book. A decision regarding what would be included in the preliminary pages, the text and the end pages, needs to be taken according to the nature of the manuscript, subject of the book and the target readers for whom the book is being written.

# 6

# Parts of a Book

## WHAT IS A BOOK?

A book is a collection of sheets of paper, parchment or other material, bound together along one edge within covers. A book is also a literary work or a main division of such a work. A book produced in electronic format is known as an e-book.

In library and information science, a book is called a monograph to distinguish it from serial publications such as magazines, journals or newspapers.

Publishers may produce low-cost, pre-proof editions known as galleys for promotional purposes, such as generating reviews in advance of publication. Galleys are usually made as cheaply as possible, since they are not intended for sale.

A lover of books is usually referred to as a bibliophile, a bibliophilist, or a philobiblist, or, more informally, a bookworm.

A book may be studied by students in the form of a book report. It may also be covered by a professional writer as a book review to introduce a new book. Some belong to a book club.

A magazine is a periodical publication containing a variety of articles, generally financed by advertising and/or purchase by readers.

Magazines are typically published weekly, biweekly, monthly, bimonthly or quarterly, with a date on the cover that is in advance of the date it is actually published. They are often printed in color on coated paper, and are bound with a soft cover.

Magazines fall into two broad categories: consumer magazines and business magazines. In practice, magazines are a subset of periodicals, distinct from those periodicals produced by scientific, artistic, academic or special interest publishers which are subscription-only, more expensive, narrowly limited in circulation, and often have little or no advertising.

## PARTS OF A BOOK

A book usually consists of three major divisions.

1. Front Matter or preliminaries (also called prelims)
2. The Text, and
3. The Back matter or End matter or Reference matter

## FRONT MATTER

Front matter or preliminary pages are numbered with lower case roman numerals. Each page is counted even though no folio (page number) is printed on display or blank pages. Right hand page is called *recto* and left hand page is called *verso.* Recto folios are odd numbered and verso folios are even numbered.

The preliminary pages may have all or some of the following item folios as part of the front matter. Some books may have lesser number of prelims depending upon the nature of the book, the author's preference and publisher's style.

Most common preliminary pages, their usual numbering and positions are:

| Page Name | Number | Position |
|---|---|---|
| *Half title page* (also called bastard title) | i | recto |
| *Back of the half title* (either blank or carries some titles or list of contributors Or frontispiece) | ii | verso |
| *Title page* | iii | recto |
| *Back of the title page* | iv | verso |
| *Dedication or epigraph* | v | recto |
| *Back of the dedication* | vi | verso |
| *Table of contents* (contents) (If dedication or epigraph is not used, Contents can start from p.v) | vii | recto |
| *List of tables or illustrations* (Depending upon the use of back of the content page) | | |

| | |
|---|---|
| *Foreword* | recto |
| *Preface* | recto |
| *Acknowledgments* (if not part of the preface) | recto |
| *Introduction* (if not part of the text) | recto |

(You can find book where introduction is given on verso)

## THE TEXT

First text page can be introduction or beginning of chapter one. Sometimes in a multi-authored book the first chapter heading is the first page. In such cases the back of the page is left blank but counted in page numbers.

*Chapters:* The text will consist of Chapters, which should be of approximately same length. Ideally each chapter should start from recto page. Chapters should display the chapter title called the running heads. In multi authored books chapter heading are sometime omitted.

*Sub Heading:* Subheads are guides for the readers if text matter is long. Subheadings should be short.

Sub-sub heading should be avoided except in scientific and technical books. Type size or style of subheadings should be different from the headings. One can use **bold** and *italic* to differentiate.

The arrangement of the text matter of a book can be as follows:

| | |
|---|---|
| *First text page*, introduction or chapter heading or chapter 1 | 1 |
| *Back of the page*, if left blank | 2 |
| *First text page* | 3 |

## BACK MATTER OR END MATTER

The material, which serves as, a reference to the text usually starts from recto page. It may have all or some of the following items depending upon the nature and size of the book.

*Appendix:* These references are given for the readers who wish to seek further information on the topic. When more than one appendix is given in a book each appendix should be given a title. Appendix can be given at the end of a chapter if it is important to the better understanding of the chapter. Text of the appendix is usually not set in small type.

*Notes:* Notes and references are given as back matter. If each chapter contains many notes and references these should be numbered chapter wise. Notes and references may be set in continuation - not necessary on the recto. Additional space is given below notes of one chapter from the other.

*Glossary:* Glossary of terms used in the text with their definition and explanation is useful tool for the readers to better understand the text. Uncommon words and phrases need to be arranged in an alphabetical order for easy finding.

*Bibliography:* The list of book consulted by the author or a list of books for further reading is usually set in small type than the text matter. This is given at the end of each chapter or becomes part of the end matter if given at the end of the text matter.

*Index:* Usually begins on a recto page and is the last item of the book. This is generally set in two columns to save space set in smaller type than the text.

*Errata:* Not a usual part of each book. Should be avoided as far as possible. Only errors severe enough to cause misunderstanding and detected too late to be rectified should be given in errata. The errors should be listed with their location with the corrected version. Extra page is inserted or tipped in if the book had already been printed or bound. It is not uncommon to place a loose sheet in the book containing errata.

The format of errata should be:

| Page | Error | Read |
|---|---|---|
| 26 | Datus Smith | Huge William |

The back matter may rendered as follows:

| | |
|---|---|
| *Appendix* | recto |
| *Notes* | recto |
| *Glossary* | recto |
| *Bibliography* | recto |
| *Index* | recto |

These are the recommended and traditionally followed arrangement of the printed matter. Any variation would depend upon the nature of the book, the publisher's preference, subject matter, author's choice and the economy factor.

# 7.

# House Style

## INTRODUCTION

House style is a set of editing and composition rules and specifications of a specific publisher, compositor and printer often codified and supplied in writing to authors and copy-editors. In house style copy-editor follows a consistent system of grammatical usage on the manuscript and a consistent, logical arrangement of the editorial components of the text—headings, subheadings, notes, quotations etc. to clarify the organisation of the book for the reader and to identify it for the printer.

It involves consistent rendering of elements of style like abbreviations, capitalisation, punctuation, word break ups and such other items where consistency can be achieved by following one set of rules. This is done to make the author's work consistent for the reader and clear and self explanatory for the printer.

There is substantial disagreement on rendering of certain elements of expression, uniform usage of which forms the basis of a house style. The job of the copy-editor is to resolve the differences and make the preferences uniform throughout the book. These preferences are, therefore, written down on a paper and called the 'style sheet' and passed on to the printer as a general guideline for printing the books of the publishing house.

These rules may all be contained on a single sheet of paper. for one publisher; another may have so many rules that a small booklet is required to accommodate them. Many publishing houses follow style bocks which provide detailed information and useful guidance in this matter. Some most sought after books are:

1. *A Manual of Style,* 13th ed. University of Chicago Press.
2. *Hart's Rules for Compositors and Readers at the University Press,* Oxford, Oxford University Press, 1978.

3. Judith Butcher, *Copy-editing,* Cambridge, Cambridge University Press, 1987.

## HOUSE STYLE VS AUTHOR'S STYLE

A house style is different from author's style of writing which usually consists of a distinctive tone, rhythm, and mode of expression that characterises the work of a particular writer, making it stand out from all other such works; envied by many writers, sought after by many editors and always a matter of individual assessment.

An author's style of writing concerns with the expression rather than the contents. Just as every singer has one's own style of singing so has every author one's own style of presenting the ideas. Each author using consistent grammatical rules may present the same theme in a different manner. This is individual to an author. This will depend upon the treatment of the subject which may be direct, compact, precise or on the contrary, indirect, verbose and pompous.

Unlike author's style of writing, a house style is a result of accuracy, appropriateness, clarity and consistency in rendering certain grammatical rules and conventions. No matter what the author's literary style is, the publisher's style would be uniform in adopting one way of presenting an item where alternatives are available. The choice of one particular usage out of many available is called the house style of a publishing house.

## PURPOSE OF HOUSE STYLE

The purpose of following a house style is to promote accuracy, speed, efficiency at the copy-editing stage to make the book well organised and consistent for the reader. It is also followed to bring out systematic portrayal of text where all such references, writings that tend to lessen the impact of the work are removed and essence of uniformity and consistency is maintained.

This is done by the arrangement of text in two ways—grammatical and typographical. Grammatical arrangement is done to clarify the organisation of the book to the reader. Typographical arrangement is done for consistent and logical rendering of the editorial components of the text for easy identification for the printer.

Some publishers have a fairly rigid style while others follow the author's style, if it is consistent. The rules differ from house to house. Unless specific instructions are given to the printer by a publisher, the printer will follow his own style or will just 'follow-copy.'

The house style, if adopted, will provide consistency in terms of spellings, form, typographical style of setting the text and other components of the manuscript, dates, titles, abbreviations and similar other items. The absence of any specific style would lead to illogical, illorganised and inconsistent reading material.

A good house style guarantees quick, accurate and honest communication. This will give the printed book elegance and distinction and would provide individualistic personality of the publishing house.

## DEVIATION FROM HOUSE STYLE

A publisher may deviate from its house style if the author has followed a consistently good style throughout the book. A rigidity in such cases may lead to confusion which the author, by following a thoroughly consistent style, though different from the publisher has tried to avoid.

In a topical book which may loose potential sale if publication is delayed, may be allowed to be printed without going into the refinement of style. A very rigid style may sometimes lead to more inconsistencies, if not minutely followed. More changes one makes in the style, the more likely one is to miss some instances and in the process the publisher may present an author with an inconsistent version of a system which the author did not choose. It is, therefore, sometimes safe to follow author's style, if consistent.

Each procedure has its own merits and demerits. If one decides to follow the author's style one has to go through the author's work to understand the author's style before the final marking up of the manuscript and the copy-editor may find himself in a fix in case where author himself is not very consistent.

## COVERAGE OF HOUSE STYLE

Consistent following of a house style will make the end product conform to the established norms of the publishing house. It will also make the manuscript easily readable and devoid of all forms of inconsistencies regarding spellings, inadequate punctuation, errors of syntax and style, the pattern of footnotes and references to bring out quality books.

1. *Abbreviations:* Do not simplify a sentence by substituting an abbreviation. Unfamiliar abbreviation should be spelt out at first occurrence. Use only standard and familiar ones. Abbreviations are used in singular form even if they are representing plural words. Avoid confusing abbreviations. Words like Mr., Mrs., Dr. etc. are always abbreviated.
2. *Capitalisation:* Capital letter should be used for proper names, parts of recognised geographical names, names of institutions and movements of history. In the quoted material first word of the direct quotation should be capitalised. Abbreviation of a proper noun should also be capitalised. Salutation and complimentary close of a letter should be capitalised. For example Dear and Sir would be capitalised if they are the beginning of the salutation. Similarly, first letter of complimentary close 'Yours faithfully' would also be capitalised.
3. *Cross references:* A reference from one page to another in a book should be clear and self explanatory. If the reference is to a page number, specific page number should be mentioned. Sectional reference should have section mark. The following abbreviations in text and footnotes are used for cross reference.

   Fig. is usually abbreviated even in text.

   Table is never abbreviated.

   pp. is used instead of p. if the reference is to more than one page.
4. *Dates and time:* There are many ways of rendering dates and time. These can be expressed in figures or in fully spelt out form. Consistency demands that one uniform system should be adopted. Dates can be expressed as follows:

   27 May 1962

   May 27, 1962

   27th May, 1962 May the 27th, 1962

   Do not mention the month every time if several dates within one month are to be given.

Use lower case letters to press a.m. and p.m. use figures to express 6.0 a.m. and words to express 6 o'clock. To express a period of time better use. 'It will take five months.' Decades are better expressed as 1980s not 1980's or '80s. If a single year comprises parts of two calendar years, it is better written with a oblique stroke between them. For example 1980/81.

5. *Footnotes:* Footnotes and bibliographic references are very important in certain books. Long footnotes should be made part of the text. Footnote should start on the same page as the text reference. Each footnote should have an indication of superscript at the end of the sentence or at the end of the particular word to which it is related.

   No important textual matter should be placed in footnotes. If several footnotes appear on one single page arrange them numerically from top to bottom. Numbering of footnotes can be done consecutively throughout the book or according to chapters. The footnotes maybe separated from the text by a solid line below the last textual line on the page.

6. *Foreign words:* Foreign words and phrases which are commonly used but not accepted as part of English language are usually italicised. They need not be italicised if they have been anglicised. Some examples of foreign words which have been anglicised are bona fide, coup, debut, gratis. Commonly used foreign phrases which have not been anglicised are: *magnum opus, coup d' etat, fait accompli.* Manuals of style usually contain list of words and phrases that are considered anglicised and which need not be italicised.

7. *Hyphenation:* Hyphen is a horizontal printed line, usually one en long, used between parts of some compound words. It is also used after first part of a broken word at the end of the line, the latter part of which is continued on the next line. It is called end of the line hyphen. It is used to separate prefix and suffix like ex-president or president-elect, to joint names or initials in some names of organizations—Park-Davis, Tata-Timkin. Hyphen is used to avoid ambiguity. Some precautions are necessary in the use of hyphen. Word break ups at the end of the line should be done according to syllables. Use of hyphen at the foot of the page should be avoided. Do not use hyphen in a set of initials (U-N-O). Any doubt in

hyphenation should be looked into a standard dictionary. Collins' *Dictionary of Spellings and Word Division* is widely used for this purpose.

8. *Italic:* Italic is a typeset at a slant to set it off from other type in the body of copy. For example *This.* Material that is to be printed in italics is underlined in typescript. The printer will automatically set the underlined material in italics unless directed otherwise. Italics are also used as emphasis device to highlight a word or phrase. Italics as emphasis device should be used sparingly otherwise you would have too many italics that it would loose its impact on the reader. Titles of books, plays, works of art, long poems are italicised. Foreign words and phrases not anglicised are also italicised. Directions to readers, *see, see also* in an index are also set in italics.
9. *Measurement and money:* The style sheet should contain preferences about rendering measurements and money.
   Statistical figures, monetary value, measurements and such special terms should be represented by numerals. It is customary to spell out numbers such as one, two, six, fifteen upto twenty and use of numerals as 21, 105 and so on. There is no hard and fast rule but it is a matter of preference. Abbreviated units of measurement have no full point and take no s in the plural e.g. 10 kg.
   Rupees can be expressed either in lakhs and crores. When whole rupee or paisa appear in the same context as fractional amount, they should be treated in a similar way, e.g. Rs. 6.00, Rs. 6.25, Rs. 0.25 and not Rs. 6, Rs. 6.25 and 25 p.
10. *Punctuation:* Punctuation is used as a safeguard against ambiguity. It should be related to the principles of good grammar. It should highlight and not confuse the meaning of the sentence. Wrong use of punctuation mark can sometime totally change the meaning of the sentence. A closer look at the sentence below will make this point clear.
    *The lion ate, Jack and Jill laughed.*
    *The lion ate Jack, and Jill laughed.*
    *The lion ate Jack and Jill, laughed.*
    Follow the author's system of punctuation, if it is consistent. Keep the punctuation marks to the minimum. Care should be taken in the use of single or double quotes around speech; use of full point

in abbreviation; use of en and em rule dash, use of ampersand '&' as a substitute for 'and'. The ellipsis (...) should be used to indicate omission of material from the quotation. Parentheses should be used for clarifying and amplifying statement to enclose a cross reference introduced in a sentence and to give additional information.

11. *Quotations:* Quotations are an integral part of the text. The author is supposed to have given his preference regarding the style in which quotations have to be displayed. Short quotation should be integrated with the sentence. Long quotations should be set off from the main text. This has been discussed under preparation of Press copy *(see* p 80).
12. *Spelling:* All words in the book should be spelled correctly. Author should be advised to be consistent with alternate spellings, like ize/ise, judgement/judgment, isation/ization. In quotations from books and articles original spellings should be retained and no effort should be made to make them consistent with the rest of the book. Watch out for words which must be spelt -ise even if the author has followed -ize pattern. Be consistent with American and British spellings. If American spellings are retained follow some good American dictionary.

The pains taken on the preparation of a house style soon pays the dividend. The copy marking can be covered by a simple instruction 'follow house style', leaving both the copy-editor and compositor or typesetter happy since they have to take very few decisions on their own. The chances are that the author's work will be faithfully reproduced in print. House style plays a major role in copy-editing the manuscript.

# 8

# Copy-Editing

Copy-editing is like nicely cooked food that is pleasant to eat and easy to digest. The person who eats is unmindful of hours of work and labour that have gone into the making of it. But when it is not done nicely, the gourmet is always critical finding faults with its taste, tang and tenderness.

## WHAT IS COPY-EDITING

Copy-editing can be defined as working over copy and preparing it for publication by improving the clarity and correctness of exposition by specifically instructing the printer on matters concerning composing or typesetting.

It is the process of word by word editing that prepares the manuscript for publication. It can also be defined as implementation of house style and looking for and providing logic, grammar and mechanism to the manuscript, before it is sent to the printer.

Copy-editing is basically mechanical marking of a manuscript so that it is in literal and literary form ready to be sent to the printer. It includes marking of the manuscript with direct instructions to the printer as to matters of style, typeface and design.

Copy-editing can be *light* which will mean little more than quick check of errors of punctuation, grammar, facts etc., or *indepth* which may include rewriting or major organisational changes in the manuscript. These changes and improvement in the manuscript can be both, qualitative and quantitative, depending upon the nature of publishing house, the author's style of writing and amiability of the copy-editor.

## PURPOSE OF COPY-EDITING

Copy-editing is done to provide homogeneity and readability to the manuscript so that errors are eliminated to make the text a pleasure to read and easy to understand. Copy-editing serves the following purposes:

1. The main purpose of copy-editing is to make the manuscript in clearest, most orderly and most effective form.
2. It enhances the publisher's reputation as producer of quality books.
3. It makes vital contribution to the quality of the final text printed by making it clear and accurate to the readers.
4. It ensures that the printed text adheres to the publisher's house style and is consistent in form and expression.
5. Copy-editing eliminates production problems at editorial stage and thereby saves the time to meet the production schedule.
6. Clearly and consistently marked copy saves the time of the compositor or typesetter.
7. Reduces corrections at proof stage because copy-edited manuscript becomes coherent, complete and accurate.
8. To see that the manuscript contains nothing which is against the law of the country and not violative of the existing copyright law of the land.
9. To provide a second eye to the author's grammar, spellings, prose and style because facts which remain hidden to author may become apparent to the copy-editor.
10. It is like showing a mirror to problems which the author has been unable to resolve may yield to the copy-editor.

## LIAISON WITH AUTHOR

A closer look at the manuscript will necessitate the need for a closer liaison with the author. It is also the job of the copy-editor to see that not only the manuscript is consistent in style, it is also complete in all respects. If it is found that something from the copy is missing, the author is contacted to provide the missing material so that a complete manuscript is sent to the printer.

Most authors do not bother for simple changes in spellings but may object at later stage if they are not informed about the kind of changes that are going to be made. Whenever changes are suggested in the manuscript, these should be supported by reasons of good grammar or style. Authors are very sensitive by nature and may object those changes in print unless informed earlier.

Copy-editor may not inform the author of every change but would win the confidence of the author if told about the nature of changes and shown examples of anticipated changes. If done so, author will not be shocked to see them at proof stage and will only mark printer's errors rather than altering the printed material and thereby creating problem of author's alteration. Author's alterations (AA's) are made by an author in composed matter, aside from corrections of printer's errors. These are usually made in galleys but sometimes in page proofs. liaison with the author reduces the incidence of author's alterations to a minimum and saves the disruption of printing schedule. It is because of such reasons that copy-editors now provide a copy of the house style to the author. A good copy-editor would settle these details with the author before the printing is started rather than after the whole work has been set in type.

## ROLE OF THE COPY-EDITOR

Communication with the reader is the aim of the author, clear communication is the job of the copy-editor. Copy-editor is a link between an author and production section. Copy-editor clarifies the text of the author's manuscript to compositor, typesetter and designer on details of production. The job of the copy-editor is to bring in uniformity and remove inconsistencies of the author's work. Though copy-editor may not be directly concerned with the contents of the text but will be responsible for the consistent presentation of the same.

## COPY-EDITOR'S CHECKLIST

There is no uniformity among the publishing houses about the nature and extent of copy-editing. No matter what limits a publishing house has set for a copy-editor, there are certain points which will always be supreme in the mind of a copy-editor if he has to ease the work of production and make a noticeable contribution to the quality of the final text.

The examination of the manuscript is done in three phases to correct errors and passages that may confuse readers and usages that may confuse the printer.

1. Preliminary stage
2. Copy-editing stage
3. Copy-marking stage

## 1. Preliminary Stage

The actual work of copy-editing begins only when it has been decided to publish a book. A good copy-editor would apply his mind on the manuscript even when the detailed copy-editing work has not started yet. This is done to save time which the copy-editor has to spend when the manuscript comes to copy-editor's desk for detailed copy-editing. Preliminary examination of the manuscript will be focussed at

1. Completeness and organisation
2. Legibility and ambiguity
3. Permissions for copyright material
4. Author's style

*Completeness and organisation*

(i) To see that the manuscript is complete in all respects.
(ii) That the text and other auxiliary material like front matter and back matter, if any, is supplied with the manuscript.
(iii) To check that no pages are missing.
(iv) Numbering of folios has been done in a logical continuous sequence.
(v) Added folios are properly numbered.
(vi) Tables, illustrations and other such material has been supplied by the author.

*Legibility and ambiguity*

(i) To see that all handwritten and typed matter is legible and easily understandable.
(ii) There is no ambiguity between O and zero, hyphen and dash, and X and multiplication sign and such other characters are easily differenciable.

*Permissions for copyright material*

(i) To see if the author has quoted extensively from other published sources whether permissions have been taken or not.
(ii) Has the author duly acknowledged the sources.
(iii) All permissions correspondence has been sent to the publisher.
(vi) That there is no possibility of copyright violation.
(v) Writing to author about this if doubts persist.

*Author's style*

(i) To take note of author's style if it is not clear, ambiguous or misleading.
(ii) To note inconsistencies, grammatical errors and factual inaccuracies.
(iii) To persuade and convince the author to make changes in harmony with the publisher's style.

2. **Copy-editing Stage**

The copy-editor will look for errors and inconsistencies and try to provide a complete, legible and unambiguous copy for the printer and a well organised, clear and consistent book for the reader. The copy-editor's work at this stage would include application of house style and watching out for:
(i) Contradictions in author's arguments
(ii) Ambiguities of ideas
(iii) Grammatical errors
(iv) Long and confusing paragraphs
(v) Parochialism
(vi) Uncommon abbreviations and terms
(vii) Spellings
(viii) Italicisation
(ix) Spacing of paragraphs
(x) Use of quotation marks
(xi) Bibliographic information, etc.
(xii) Coding and numbering of illustrations
(xiii) Footnotes and information
(xiv) Appendices

### 3. **Copy marking stage**

In order to provide a complete, self-explanatory copy for the printer, the copy-editor marks the press copy with instructions to ensure understanding of the requirement by the compositor. The typescript is marked with dear and unambiguous instructions and symbols so that each and every part of the manuscript is dearly understandable by the compositor so that the printer can start his work of composing or typesetting without having to stop to think what the author meant to write. The copy-editor at this stage instructs the printer about:

(i) Type size and style
(ii) Position of fresh page
(iii) Text to be set in different type size
(iv) Choice of quotation marks
(v) Instructions about placement of illustrations etc.
(vi) Positioning of Headings, subheadings
(vii) Footnotes and endnotes
(viii) Glossary and Index

## MARKING THE MANUSCRIPT

The golden rule for marking the press copy is that whatever is marked, should be dear and marked throughout the manuscript. The copy-editor should copy-edit the manuscript and not proof read it. All corrections should be marked in the interlinear space and only instructions to the printer should be written in the margin and ringed. This would mean that matter within the circle is only an instruction and not an addition in the manuscript.

Words and passages which are to be typographically distinguished should be dearly indicated. The following symbols are commonly used to indicate variations in printing an item.

(i) A single line drawn beneath a word or sentence would mean that the matter is to be composed in *italics.*
(ii) A wavy line calls for a **bold face.**
(iii) For indicating SMALL CAPITALS two lines are given beneath the word or words.

(iv) Three straight lines are used for instructing CAPITAL LEITERS.

(v) Three straight lines below the first letter and two beneath the remaining part of the word would mean first letter to be capital and remaining part to be in lower case letters also called CAPITALS and SMALL CAPITALS.

(vi) *ITALIC CAPITAL* is shown by four lines below the matter to be composed as such.

(vii) BOLD CAPITALS would be directed by three straight lines and a wavy line below them.

The following examples show the marking on the manuscript and the desired results in composed matter.

| *Marking on the Typescript* | *Instructions to printer* | *Matter to be set as* |
|---|---|---|
| *BOOK PUBUSHING* | Italics | *Book Publishing* |
| BOOK PUBUSHING | Bold face | **Book Publishing** |
| BOOK PUBLISHING | Small Capitals | BOOK PUBLISHING |
| BOOK PUBLISHING | Capitals | BOOK PUBLISHING |
| BOOK PUBLISHING | Capital and Small Capital | BOOK PUBLISHING |
| BOOK PUBLISHING | Capital italics | *BOOK PUBLISHING* |
| BOOK PUBLISHING | **Bold face capitals** | **BOOK PUBLISHING** |

(viii) In order to indicate a passage which is to be set in different type size, a vertical line is drawn alongside the passage from the beginning till the end of the material to be set in different type size.

(ix) Headings should be coded to indicate their position. For example [A] for headings and [B] for subheadings. The coding should be given in squares.

(x) Any addition of word or words should be made by using a 'λ' caret mark at the appropriate place. Do not write in the margin.

(xi) For deletion, just delete the letter or word by using ℘ deletion sign.

(xii) Transposition—to reverse or otherwise change to proper order is done by using transposition mark ⊔⊓

(xiii) Stet mark - - - - is used to retain the - - - - - - - word or words.

(xiv) For close up use ⊂ sign.

(xv) For joining paragraphs ⟶ is used

(xvi) If a capital letter is to be changed into a lower case letter, use a diagonal line through the capital letter. Book Publishing.

## DO'S AND DONT'S OF A COPY-EDITOR

1. Do not re-write or change the text.
2. Do not hesitate to ask the author for any clarification.
3. Mark the manuscript throughout and not in patches.
4. Do not proof read but copy-edit the manuscript.
5. Do not overwrite.
6. Follow author's style, if consistent.
7. Change with caution. (National/Notional), (Casual/Causal), (College/Collage).
8. Respect the author. Listen, if the author persists on a point.
9. Do not hesitate to put your point firmly.
10. All decisions regarding manuscript should be recorded.

## TOOLS OF THE COPY-EDITOR

"An editor is a person", says Samuel Israel "who reads with a pencil in hand". Pencil, therefore, is the simplest and most important tool of the copy-editor. Other things which are indispensible in the performance of good copy-editing work include:

1. Standard language dictionary/encyclopedia.
2. Style manual.
3. Pens of different colour to differenciate between corrections and instructions.
4. Erasers and correction fluid.
5. Numbering machine to give consecutive pagination.

# 9

# Preparation of Press Copy

## DEFINITION

Press copy can be defined as a manuscript ready to be set into type-text, photographs, drawings and other materials-infact anything that is to form part of the book, ready to be sent to the printer. It also means putting instructions on manuscript to ensure understanding of the requirement by the compositor. It is to ensure that the manuscript is grammatically correct and that rendering of capitalisation, spellings, punctuation mark, word break ups and other requirements of linguistic structure are taken care of.

Before the manuscript is given for typing, the editor or author should ensure that the manuscript is complete in all respects. Various elements of the manuscript should be collected and arranged in an order so that they are typed in a sequence without any gaps in the continuity of the manuscript. This orderly arrangement will help the typist to type without halts to collect left out material. This will also save time and eliminate the chances of anything being left out in the final draft.

## PARTS OF THE MANUSCRIPT

A complete manuscript can be divided into three parts:

1. Preliminary or Front matter
2. Body of the manuscript or Text matter
3. End matter or back matter.

*Front matter:* All items to be printed preceding the main text of the book including the title page, copyright information, table of contents, list of illustrations, list of tables, dedication, preface, foreword including other information pages not part of the body of the text, form part of the preliminary pages or front matter. It is the responsibility of the author to provide these items. If the author has not done so, it is the job of the editor to remind him to do so. Some books may have more and others may have lesser number of pages that form part of the front matter. Whether an item is considered front matter or back matter (matter that comes after the body of the text) will be dependent upon its placement in a publication. These pages are numbered with lower case roman numerals.

*Text matter* or *Body of the manuscript:* The body of the manuscript or contents of a work, as set forth in words, not including the front matter or back matter and non word composition, such as illustrations is called the text of the manuscript. Text contains organisation of various chapters. Numbering of the text should begin with arabic numerals from the first page of the introduction. If the paging is being done according to chapters, indication of chapter number in upper case roman should also be given on the manuscript so that pages do not get mixed up with other chapters.

*Back matter or End matter:* Everything that follows the main text of a manuscript including such materials as glossaries, appendices, footnotes, bibliographies etc. are grouped as back matter. As mentioned earlier, if such materials appear in the body of the text except index, they become part of the text. Both back matter and front matter are identified by placement within a manuscript rather than by form or content. Back matter is also known as end matter. Back matter is listed with page numbers on the contents page. Care should be taken that all references notes, footnotes etc. forming part of the back matter, have proper corresponding information to link them with the main text.

## ROLE OF THE TYPIST

The role of the typist is of great significance in the preparation of press copy. A poorly typed manuscript will be full of errors and erasures, sure to cause confusion at the time of typesetting the matter. Preparation of manuscript also means putting instructions on manuscript to ensure understanding of the requirements by the compositor. This will be possible only if an efficient and accurate typist is employed to type the manuscript. Carefully typed matter would minimise the chances of mistakes in the final printing.

An expert and accurate typist with thorough knowledge of basics of typewriting, like centering the page, providing uniform margin, maintaining length and number of lines, erasing and correcting the wrong strokes and proper use of correction fluid, should be employed for the job. If more than one person is doing the typing the same instructions and guidelines, as to how to type the manuscript, should be given to each one of them. The manuscript should be typed on the same machine throughout the entire text. This makes the work of casting off—estimating the length of the manuscript when typeset, easier and near accurate.

Needless to say that the entire manuscript should be typed in double space and only on one side of the paper. Not only it is difficult to read single space matter, it is also difficult to add in between the lines if the matter has not been typed double spaced. Double space means a full blank line between all typed lines, not just between notes and items of bibliography but in the entire manuscript which is to be printed. Typing on one side of the paper eliminate the chances of a portion either composed for the second time or not composed at all.

*Corrections:* No matter who does the typing, the author or the typist, it is always better to give a quick look to the typed page to detect any error before the page is removed from the machine. This would avoid retyping of pages and also efforts to realign the copies with carbon. Because once the paper has been removed, it is very time consuming and cumbersome to realign the strokes of the typewriter on the page.

## CHECKLIST

Some publishers maintain a checklist which they pass on to authors so that the manuscript is received in a form which is ready to be sent to the printer. The neatness with which the copy has been prepared will go a longway in helping the printer to do his work more efficiently. The checklist coupled with a sense of responsibility on the part of the author and the copy editor will make the copy presentable and usually include the following points.

*Paper:* The manuscript should be typed on a good quality paper preferably on 8.5½ x 11 inches in size. The paper should be stout with good erasing qualities. Because, if the paper is not strong enough it may not withstand the handling by the compositor who has to fold it not once but many times in the process of compositing or typesetting the matter. The poor quality of paper would leave eraser marks which may reduce the legibility of the typed matter. Strong use of eraser may even tear off the portion thus spoiling the page.

The entire manuscript should be typed on a uniform size of paper and preferably of the same quality. The uniform size would enable the production department to make near exact estimate of the number of pages the book will have when printed in a particular type and book size.

*Ribbon and Carbon:* The typing should be done only on one side of the paper with fresh ribbon and carbon. The ribbon and carbon should be replaced when impression starts becoming light. Overuse of typewriter ribbon can give very light impression. To avoid this one can use carbon ribbon—a special quality ribbon which is used only once and gives an even quality of typing impression. Do not overtype on a wrongly typed word or sentence. Strike out the incorrect word or sentence and retype the corrected version. Use a good quality eraser to make shorter corrections. While using eraser care should be taken to avoid eraser marks on the carbon copies. Ribbon copy *i.e.* the direct typewriter impression and not the carbon copy, should be made the press copy.

*Margins:* Sufficient margins on the top, left and bottom should be left while typing the manuscript. Usually margin on the left is more than the margin on the top and bottom. Preferably leave margin on the left of about 4 cm and about 2.5 cm at the top and bottom. Sometimes it is difficult to maintain uniform margin on the right side on a manual typewriter.

*Word Division:* An effort to maintain the right side margin should not be used as an excuse for large number of word break ups at the end of the line. Word division should be done sensibly and when a word can not be included without entering too deep into the right margin and syllable break up is also disturbing the margin, the entire word should be taken to the next line. Too many word break ups at the end of the line give a clumsy appearance. Hyphenated words should be broken at the hyphen. One should try to avoid one letter or two letter divisions, such as O-nce, e-vil and us-age. One should not hesitate to consult a standard reference work to decide a proper word break up in case of doubt.

*Illustrations:* Like tables and other text material, illustrations are not typeset but are reproduced from artwork prepared by the artist. They include graphs, charts, photos, paintings, drawings etc. It is advised not to pin or clip in the originals alongwith the manuscript. Nothing should be written on the artwork. Since these are not typeset, each illustration should be suitably numbered indicating the figure number and the corresponding page number in the text to which it belongs.

Just as tables, one can indicate with two horizontal lines and a note therein where one thinks the illustration should be placed. Alternately, encircled note in the margin should indicate the location of the exact position of the illustration or drawing. These may also be numbered in one consecutive series or according to chapters.

Authors should keep a copy of each of the illustration or drawing with their serial number and caption. While sending the artwork to the printer. Care should be taken so that the illustrations and other drawings do not bend, spindle or mutilate.

*Quotations:* A quotation can be defined as a statement directly attributed to its originator. Quotations are used by authors to convey information and to substantiate a point of view by using words of some expert or authority on the subject under reference. A quotation should be accurately reproduced and sources verified. Directly quoted material should be faithfully reproduced in all its details including spellings, capitalisation, punctuation marks and paragraphing.

Quoted material, small in length may become part of the sentence using single quote mark. Long quotations should be indented four or five spaces so that matter may be set in type narrower than the full line measure. Very long quotations are sometimes shortened by using ellipsis. An ellipsis consists of three spaced periods (...) The matter to be set in type indented form should be typed indented. Quoted material should also be typed in double space.

*Footnotes:* Authors usually acknowledge the sources of ideas and information to authenticate their view point. This is credited either within the text matter or separately as footnotes. A footnote is a citation at the bottom of the page giving credit for ideas or statements taken from published material or other sources. Footnotes are sometimes given to explain the main text matter. These are used to acknowledge the fact quoted, to support the author's argument, to give reference to material quoted elsewhere in the manuscript and to give additional information on a given idea or concept.

A consistent pattern of footnotes be used throughout the manuscript to make the accessibility of the cited source easy. A footnote citation should usually include (1) the name of the author, (2) the title of the book, (3) details of the publication and location of the information referred. For example

Datus C. Smith (Jr.), *A Guide to Book Publishing* (New York: Bowker, 1966), p. 8.

In case the reference is cited for the second time on the same page or some other page, certain abbreviations are used. Most commonly used abbreviations are:

1. *Ibid:* Abbreviated form of the word *Ibidem,* which in Latin stands for 'in the same place', is used for consecutive reference to the same source in order to avoid repetition. Robert Escarpit, *The Book Revolution* (London, Harrap, 1966) p.23.
   *Ibid.* p.25.
2. *Op. Cit.:* This is the abbreviated form of the latin word *Opere citato.* When references are made to the same work following each other closely but not consecutively and when they refer to different pages *op.cit.* is used in a series of footnotes with the author's name, making unnecessary the repetition of all information about the work in question. This is used after the first entry in place of title and details of publication.
3. *Loc Cit:* It is used with non consecutive footnotes that refer to the same work and to the same page(s). It usually requires the author's name but omits the page number.

*Examples*

Robert Escarpit, *The Book Revolution* (London, Harrap, 1966), p. 23.

*Ibid.* p,25.

Datus C. Smith (Jr.), *A Guide to Book Publishing* (New York, Bowker, 1966), p.224.

Escarpit, *Op.cit.,* p. 28.

Smith (Jr.) *Loc cit.*

*Subheadings:* A subheading is a heading on the body of copy, such as a chapter sub section, usually to be set in type different from that used in the body of the copy and often larger and bolder than the copy, but subordinate in size and placement to such mainheads as titles and chapter and section heading. They are used to break up the long chapter and highlight the different areas discussed in that chapter. Judicious use of subheadings serves as a guide to readers.

Indiscriminate use of subheadings can be very confusing. A proper thought over this area of text presentation, therefore, is required both by the authors as well as the editors. Subheadings should be planned before the process of writing begins. An intelligent use of subheadings would help the author to outline the structure of his work and broad contents of each section. Subheadings should be short, succinct and meaningful.

The position of subheadings should be levelled and their position should be indicated by degree of the level. The level would also indicate the status of the subheading.

*Pagination:* Pages should be numbered in strict sequence. Any pages deleted must be struck through but retained in the typescript if the numbering has been done. Additional pages of copy should be marked A, B etc. and attached to the previous sheet of copy, and a clear indication at appropriate page should be given about the extra material. For example if a page is added to page number 20 it should carry a line, followed by 20A and page 21 should have the indication that it follows page number 20A. So that there is no confusion for the typist and the typesetter.

*Other Guidelines:* Whoever is entrusted the work of preparing the press copy, should be consistent in choice of spellings, italicisation of foreign words and phrases. Any diacritical marks not on a typewriter on which the manuscript has been typed should be marked in ink carefully and consistently. Margins are not to be used for corrections. When adding a short word or phrase, indicate it by a caret (λ) mark where it should appear. All corrections and additions should be made in legible hand.

It is difficult to maintain consistency unless you have some source to depend upon. There are many standard style books available in the market. It is worthwhile to buy one or two to enrich your reference shelf.

Last but not the least, the decision whether the making of the press copy should be done on the copy supplied by the author or it has to be retyped, should be taken before setting your hands for marking the press copy for the printer.

## PRECAUTIONS

1. Do not proof read the copy. Copy edit it. Do not mark the corrections in margins. Use the inter lineal space for this purpose. This explains why typing should be double spaced.
2. Do not bind the press copy as binding may have to be broken up for composing and typesetting.
3. Do not overwrite on the typematter. X out the word and type the new word.
4. Do not pin or clip the papers. This will leave holes in the manuscript.
5. Do not fold or roll sheets of paper in the manuscript.
6. Do not fasten or attach a typed passage or revised matter without giving it a separate page number.

# 10

# Pre Press

Before the advent of the computer aided soft wares to do the pre presswork, the typesetter used to receive the manuscript prepared with printing specification from the production department. The typesetting was done by typecasting machines (discussed in chapter on Methods of Composing). The matter thus composed was sent to the paste up person who would put it on the paste up board along with other elements of the document to be printed.

These images were then photographed, cropped, enlarged or reduced as per design format using photographic process the photographed matter was placed on the paste up board where images would appear. Once the text and other elements are in place on the paste up board, the negatives of all the images were made to size. these paste up sheets were checked for any correction. These sheets were imposed- arranged in order in which they were to be printed. The imposed pages were made into plates from which the document was printed on paper on the printing press.

Copy editing, typesetting, designing, page layout proof reading, screening of tone of images such as photographs, retouching the page assembly, imposition (arrangements of order in which the pages were to be printed) trapping-also called spreading and choking, colour separation and plate making (photomechanical exposure and processing of light-sensitive emulsion on a printing plate) etc, were considered part of the pre press process.

## NEED OF TIME

In the last quarter of twentieth century computer aide prepress techniques began to supplement and in some cases replace the traditional darkroom and light table processes described above. In the beginning of this century the word prepress became almost synonymous with digital prepress. Before that, prepress workers were involved in preparation of negatives and printing plates for use on the press. Prepress workers might still in some places be doing typesetting and page composing; however, as digital prepress technology has become less costly, more efficient and reliable, and as the knowledge and skill required to use the new hardware and especially software have become more widespread within the production staff, digital route has been introduced to almost every part of the process.

Today's prepress workers will sort out electronically 'strip' your pages together, do color correction before the piece is on the press, fix any compositional errors or problems, and create a digital file that will then be made into a negative or sent directly to a printing plate.

## WHAT IS PREPRESS?

Prepress is the term used in the printing and publishing industries for the processes and procedures that occur between the procurement of a written manuscript and original artwork, and the manufacture of a printing plate, image carrier, or (traditionally) forme, ready for mounting on a printing press.

Before the advent of the computer and print related soft wares like Page Maker and laser printers, a large number of jobs were required to be done on the copy edited manuscript and many people with various caliber were required to do different jobs before a page could be sent to the press. Prepress work now begins after the design decisions are made and ends when the document reaches the press

## PREPRESS DEFINED

This is the process of preparing a print job for the actual printing process. Although the term can be used to refer to everything from photography and graphic design to copyediting and typesetting, it is generally used to refer to the things that need to happen to get the job into the press.

Prepress refers to the preparation of digital files for printing. It comes after the design and page layout stage, although prepress planning is crucial during those stages to insure that files print properly.

In typography and printing, prepress stands for the preparation of camera-ready materials up to the actual printing stage, which includes typesetting, page makeup and plate processing. By the turn of the century, the creation of digital content by authors and designers, digital printers, computer-to-plate (CTP) technologies and direct image (DI) presses all contributed to dramatically shortening the prepress cycle.

## DEFINITIONS OF PREPRESS

The preparation work required to turn camera-ready or digital artwork into the printing plates needed for mass production, ie, making negatives.

The production steps before printing, particularly those steps needed to transform the original copy into the printing plates or other form needed for reproduction (ie stripping, image setting, proofing, plate making).

The process of getting an image ready to go on press. Digital prepress denotes the entire preparation of a digital file for printing in either a digital or conventional system.

The various steps necessary to prepare a book to be sent to a printer. May include scanning of images, creation of proofs, conforming color specifications to the printer's requirements, and many other activities.

In order to understand the prepress work, we should know the processes and equipment needed in prepress operation.

*Camera:* An apparatus for taking photographs, generally consisting of a lightproof enclosure having an aperture with a shuttered lens through which the image of an object is focused and recorded on a photosensitive film, plate, or sensor.

*Stripping:* (In printing) is a dying trade in which film negatives are arranged in a pattern, which will create a series of pages. There is an individual negative for each color to be printed on a printing press. Colors are arranged in order to fit together with the other colors to be printed. This process has generally been eliminated through the use of digital prepress, in which imposition software is used to "digitally strip" the pages together. The digital product of this software can be outputted to an image setter that creates larger piece of film, or directly to a plate setter, which generates a plate that can go directly to press.

*Pre-flighting:* This is just like checking all the items you need before you leave your home for travel. This term is used in the printing industry to describe the process of confirming that the digital files required for the printing process are all present, valid, correctly formatted, and of the desired type.

*Negative image:* In larger cameras this piece of film may be as large as a full sheet of paper, or even larger, with a single image captured onto one piece. Each of these negative images may be referred to as a *negative* and the entire strip or set of images may be collectively referred to as negatives. These negative images are the master images, from which all other copies will be made, and they are treated with care and handled with caution. A positive image is a normal image. A *negative image* is a tonal inversion of a positive image, in which light areas appear dark and vice versa. A negative color image is additionally color reversed, with red areas appearing cyan, greens appearing magenta and blues appearing yellow

*Colour management:* It is the controlled conversion between the color representations of various devices, such as image scanners, digital cameras, monitors, TV screens, film printers, computer printer, offset presses, and corresponding media. The main aim of color management is to obtain a good match across color devices. Color management helps to achieve the same appearance on all of these devices, provided the devices are capable of delivering the needed color intensities

*Digital camera:* It is an electronic device used to capture and store photographs digitally, instead of using photographic film like conventional cameras, or recording images in an analog format to magnetic tape like many video cameras. Since the technology produces a graphics file, the image can be readily edited using suitable software.

*Computer printer:* It is an electronic device that accepts text files or images from a computer and transfers them to a medium such as paper or film. It can be connected directly to the computer or indirectly via a network. Computer printer, or more commonly a printer, produces a hard copy (permanent human-readable text and/or graphics) of documents stored in electronic form, usually on physical print media such as *paper* or transparencies. In addition, many modern printers can directly interface to electronic media such as memory sticks or memory cards, or to image capture devices such as digital cameras and scanners.

Some printers are combined with a scanner and/or fax machine in one unit.

*Desktop Publishing*, or *DTP:* It is the term applied to the process of creating and publishing professional-looking documents using microcomputers. DTP systems can produce many types of documents, from simple to sophisticate, including business cards, letterheads, stationery, brochures, newsletters, flyers, maps, coupons, posters, invitations, business graphics, annual reports, proposals, and magazines. For such projects, a company would need photography equipment, photo-editing software, illustration software, and page-layout software. (more details on DTP given in chapter on Methods of Composing)

*Press proof* is a proof from the printing press, plates, and actual inks specified for the job. A press proof is used to verify images, tone values, colors, and imposition. Because it involves setting up the job and running a proof on the actual paper to be used, it is normally done with the designer on-site (and sometimes your customer as well). It's your last chance to get it right and can add additional cost to the job. A press proof is generally done in lieu of a prepress contract proof.

*Prepress proof*: It is an analog or digital proof that uses inkjet, toner, dyes, overlays, photographic film, or other techniques to give a close approximation of what the finished piece will look like. Unlike a press proof, the prepress proof does not use the actual printing inks, therefore, color proofs may not be quite as accurate as a press proof. Analog prepress proofs include inexpensive contact proofs such as blue lines, used for checking positioning or where exact color is less critical; and, more expensive but increasingly accurate color overlay and laminate proofs. While analog prepress proofs use photographic or film techniques, digital prepress proofs print directly from the digital files to inkjet, laser, and similar printers.

*Overlay:* By printing each color separation of a file on a clear overlay material each color can be proofed separately or superimposed on each other to proof the entire page. Overlay proofs are created from the film separation that places each ink color on a separate clear acetate sheet or film material then stacks them together in alignment (registered) over white paper or other substrate.

*Cromacheck* and *Color Key* overlay proofs are two brands of overlay proofing systems.

These are also known as dry proof/off-press proof/digital CMYK proof/continuous tone proof/halftone proof.

*Plate setter:* A machine that generates plates for a printing press. A plate setter is similar in function to an image setter, except that instead of producing film from which the plates are made, the plates themselves are made. *See CTP.*

*Image setter:* A machine that generates output for the printing process, which is either a film-based paper that is photographed or the actual film for making the printing plates. Input comes from the keyboard, or via disk, tape or modem. Earlier machines handled only text and were called "phototypesetters." Most imagesetters today support the PostScript language.

*PostScript (PS)* is a dynamically typed concatenative programming language created by John Warnock and Charles Geschke in 1982. PostScript is best known for its use as a page description language in the electronic and desktop publishing areas.

## COMPUTER-TO-PLATE (CTP)

The production of printing plates directly from the computer without requiring film as an intermediate step is called "direct-to-plate". The plates are typically made of aluminum, but polyester, polymer and silicon plates are also used. Off-press imaging refers to using a plate setter to create the plates and then manually attaching the plates on the press. In on-press imaging, or direct imaging (DI), images plates that are already on the press. In.

The term computer-to-plate indicates printing directly from digital files. Since all computer printers are computer-to-press, it could refer to a large digital printer. It could also refer to an on-press computer-to-plate machine. It would not refer to off-press computer-to-plate

In the Computer-to-Plate or CTP process the image of the page from a digital file is recorded directly from the file to the printing plate instead of creating film and making the plate from the film. Although CTP is a printing process, in order to insure the best possible output it is important that the designer discusses CTP with their printer. The printer's familiarity with the process, their equipment, the type of plates, and file format and preparation, all play a major role in the success of the computer-to-plate process

*D I Press:* DI, or Direct Imaging, is the process of sending a digital file directly to a press without the use of traditional offset or computer-to-plate processes or chemistry. DI presses eliminate the production steps and variables normally associated with off-press plate making processes. A DI press allows a printer to be more competitive—and profitable—in a market that continually demands faster turnaround times, shorter press runs, and expects lower cost without sacrificing quality.

Prepress is basically a production job, as it requires the book design to be finalized before prepress work starts on a manuscript. In certain publishing organizations prepress is part of the processing unit of the editorial department.

# 11

# List Development

Publishing is an integral part of the intellectual and cultural system of any country. Most simply the publisher is a coordinator of the process by which a book is produced. "A publisher is, therefore," writes Philip G. Altback, "a businessman, an intellectual, a publicity agent, a grammarian and hopefully in the long run a teacher." Publishers also directly influence the content of what is written. The most pervasive and direct way the publisher can influence this, is to conceive of a work himself and commission an author to write it. In the process of publishing this work of creating ideas into books is the responsibility of the editor.

## LIST DEFINED

List can be defined as all of publishers books in print and for sale. This includes all titles a publisher carries in print other than those published recently, usually within six months or so. Some publishers treat books as new—current list (also called front list) for considerably longer than six months or so with back list classification reached only after sales or topical interests have subsided.

The list of a publisher can be classified into three categories:

1. *Current* List: As books currently being published and on sale, published during the recent past. These are new and almost new books on publisher's list, usually those of single publishing season; but some publishers include books generated in previous season as current list if they are worthy of sustained promotion.

2. *Back List*: As books which have been published in the past one or more years though some of them may still be available on sale. Strength of the back list, that is, salability of the books published in the previous years, is one of the critical factors affecting the continuing profit of the publisher and continuing service to public interest. For many publishers back list is

the key to success through the years, a 'badge of pride and a source of continuous income.'

3. *Future List*: As list of books already contracted and which may be made available for sale in the near future. Sometimes books under printing are also included in the future list.

## LIST DEVELOPMENT

The systematic planning, scheduling and converting book ideas into books and making them available to readers is called list development. The development of the list is the main responsibility of the editorial department though the entire publishing house, in some way or the other, will be connected with it. Samuel Israel describes list development as "To acquire, for a publishing house, in a planned and purposeful manner, and on a continuing basis, material for publication in book form that will meet an existing, anticipated and potential need; and that can be made available in economic quantities at prices acceptable to those requiring or interested in the material."

## EDITOR'S ROLE

The editor who is to shoulder the prime responsibility of the development of the publisher's list has to make continuous efforts to acquire manuscripts which can be converted into book projects and that this acquisition has to be made in a planned manner. Planning means keeping in view the finances available at publisher's disposal and the assessment of the needs of the market for that kind of a book. The acquisition of book idea must fulfill some purpose, give adequate return to the publisher and fill the information gap in the market so that there are ready buyers of the book. Unless these precautions are taken, the editor will end up with a list which is undistinguished and with no promise of sustained profit to the publishing house.

Publishing is a business which is ten times more unpredictable than any other business. The editor has to use his sixth sense to predict how many copies may be printed in the first instance and will also prophecy the probable sales to arrive a at decision about economic edition, not forgetting that publishers are always haunted by the ghost of over printing or under printing. In both situations, publisher stands to loose. That is why publishing is called a business with 'gambling instinct.'

There must, therefore, be books that are sure of wide, quick, immediate sale and those, which with a smaller original sale, will become established and, perhaps, sell for many years. No publishing house can really be successful without building such a treasure house of back list books. It is also said in publishing circle that a good backlist works while you sleep.

## CONTINUOUS PROGRAMME

The main pressure for a publisher to remain in publishing is to have a continuous flow of books. What publishers feel is not only the pressure for more profits but need for growth, expansion and more books. It is easy to become a publisher, but difficult to remain one, because 'mortality rate at infancy in this profession is very high.'

List development, therefore, demands that publishing programme of a publishing house should be planned in a manner that energies of the staff are not over exercised for a particular period of the year and remain idle during the rest of the year. This is done by choosing the field of publishing most appropriate and rewarding for a particular publishing house in a particular set of circumstances and setting out for the acquisition of the kind of manuscripts required to fill the bill in a regular flow 'neither drought nor flood' is what list development is all about.

The editor's job is to convert the dream of publishing salable books into a reality. The editor has to work relentlessly so that the flow of manuscripts does not slop. The editor needs to remain constantly alert and sensitive to market needs and strive for the availability of authors who can not only fulfill the need but also provide the manuscript within the prescribed time schedule. The result of this would be a perfectly planned and executed list.

Editor's job does not finish there. As John Farrar puts it "It has been a successful season. The editor may relax but only briefly, for he must begin to dream of the next season and the next."

# Part III
# Production Department—Producing the Book

# 12
# Methods of Composing

Composing can be defined as the process of setting the type or assembling by hand or machine individual pieces of type which are cast on type casting machines or which are supplied to the printer by a type founder. It is the process of assembling characters, figures, symbols, signs and spaces to make words and paragraphs in the required type size and page measure.

Methods of composing can be broadly divided into the following four categories:

1. Hand composing
2. Mechanical or Hot metal composing
3. Cold composing or Photo mechanical methods
4. Desk Top Publishing

### 1. *Hand Composing or Manual Typesetting*

Hand composing is a very conventional method of arranging matter by hands. With the introduction of new unconventional methods of composing matter into type like photo-typesetting and Desk Top Publishing, hand composing has been relegated to jobs like printing of letter heads, visiting cards, bill books and such other small printing works. Though speed is not on the side of hand composing but the economy of process and the ability to set at one time a range of varying sizes or different styles of type make it a favoured method in similar jobs. Hand composing is also useful where large and varied characters are required.

The type that a compositor uses is stored in a shallow box called a *case.* It is a metal type storage case, traditionally holding two drawers, the upper for the capital or upper case and the lower for small or lower case letters. These cases are usually made of wood. There are several compartments of different sizes to hold types and spaces etc.

The compositor picks up a single type from the composing case and places it on the *composing stick*a—piece of compositor's equipment. Compositor's stick is a three sided tray made of metal and used for setting lines of type. It is called a stick because originally it used to be made of wood. The tray is about 9" long by 2" wide by ½" deep and has a sliding head that can be fixed to any desired width either by a screw or by a lever.

The stick is kept in left hand with the head set to the desired length of the line. Letters and characters are placed one after the other and the process of lifting and placing characters in a desired sequence continues until the whole line or paragraph is complete or composing stick fills up.

Thus composed lines of type are transferred to a long shallow tray meant for holding composed matter. Such tray is called a *galley.* Proofs drawn from such trays from uncorrected copy set in a single column of any width, prior to page make up, are called galley proofs.

By assembling various elements of type, display type, rules, cuts etc. according to the page layout, pages are made up. In a small job pages can be made up on galleys. In case of book work it may be made up on imposing table. This is done by tying up the type with a string and securely locking up the composed matter. The locking up can be done either on the galley or in a metal frame called a *chase* or directly on the bed of the press.

The locked matter which is ready for printing or taking out proofs is called a *form.* After these proofs have been taken, corrections are also made by hand, removing the wrong letter or character and replacing it with the correct one.

The corrected matter is then finally printed. The type is cleaned and distributed back into the case and individual letters are kept back in their respective compartments for future use. Care needs to be taken while distribution otherwise numerous mistakes will occur when type is reused for composing. The process of hand composing is slow and has become too expensive for lengthy typesetting jobs.

2. *Mechanical or Hot Metal Composing*

With the spread of education and interaction between nations, hand composing method could not keep pace with the demand for the printed word. Innovators were trying to build machines which could overcome the handicaps of hand composing.

With the introduction of monotype and linotype in the last decade of the nineteenth century, the composing methods underwent revolutionary change. Since the type in both the methods is cast from a hot metal, therefore, such composing is also known as 'hot metal composing'. These machines not only assemble type, but create it afresh from molten metal.

There are four major type casting methods:

(i) *Monotype:* A trade name of a machine that casts lines of type out of hot metal in single characters.

(ii) *Linotype:* It casts line of types in a single slug created from hot metal.

*(iii) Intertype:* It produces lines of type as in linotype.

*(iv) Ludlow Caster:* Produces type from 12 point to 72 points.

### (i) *Monotype*

The monotype machine was invented by Talbot Lanston. The first such machine was produced in London in 1889. As the name indicates, in this system single character composing can be done not in lines and slugs. It is, therefore, also called 'single letter composing machine'. The main innovative features of the machine were justified composed line and the use of paper tape to drive a casting and composing machine.

The monotype system comprises of two distinct parts or machines (i) key board and (ii) caster—The first perforates a roll of paper with holes in a pattern forming a set of instructions; the second casts letters, figures and spaces in metal according to the instructions.

*Keyboard:* Keyboard of a monotype machine is similar to that of a typewriter and characters are arranged in the same manner. But the keyboard is divided into a few key banks such as key bank, bar bank, rock shaft and justification drum and stop bar etc.

The keyboard has upto seven alphabet layout. The operator can pick any character from these alphabets in one family and size only. Any matter to be composed in different typeface or size must be keyed and cast separately and made up manually on the imposition stone.

Above the key board is a roll of paper which is fed from one spool to another an eighth of an inch at a time as each character is completed. Below the spool of paper there are 31 punches. When a key is pressed it releases compressed air which actuates two valves; two punches rise to perforate the paper.

At the same time as the codes are punched the width of the characters which have been punched, is registered adding it to the total of the letters already in the line and a mechanism known as justifying drum indicates to the operator the space which remains in the line. As the end of the line approaches, the mechanism calculates the correct amount of space necessary to justify the line. The operator needs only to press the indicated justification key and the line is complete. A key resets the pointer and a new line is started. When the last line has been keyed and justified the perforated paper is taken to the caster.

Further development to monotype keyboard is the Duplex keyboard. Duplex keyboard has two paper rolls instead of one and also punches two spools at a time. Though the principle of working is the same, the duplex keyboard can do the same job in single operation in two different typefaces, type sizes and measures.

*Monotype Caster:* After the whole matter to be set in type has been keyed, the perforated roll is taken to the caster which produces single metal types corresponding to the letters keyed on the keyboard.

The main elements of a caster are a matrix case with 255 characters, (225 and 272 character matrices are also available) a mould and a wedge. These parts together give each face its appropriate body and justification, wedges alter the space between words.

The perforated paper is placed on the type caster where compressed air mechanism reads the perforation, causing pins to move the draw rods which control the movement of the mould. The air passing through the perforations brings the matrix holder, and the specified matrix ready to be filled with molten metal, into proper position.

The mould is water cooled and as the metal solidifies, the excess is cut off at the foot and a piece of newly cast type is ejected into a channel. By the same process the types accumulate in the channel until the line is complete. It then ejects the complete line into a galley.

Monotype composing caster can set type from 4¼ point to 14 point in any measure upto 36 picas. Display matter to accompany monotype setting is normally set by hand by types cast on a super caster which works on the same principles and can cast upto 72 points.

Monotype provides a very high standard in mechanical composing. It is regarded very useful for those jobs where quality of typesetting is of great importance.

It is ideal for complex setting such as tables, charts, scientific and mathematical materials. It is widely used for text books.

Monotype composing sets each character separately. Individual elements in a line may be corrected by using pre cast sorts out of the type case without having to reset the entire line. Monotype can set type and leading as one piece. One great advantage of monotype composing is the ease with which corrections can be carried out. However, it is possible to increase the leading, but not reduce it.

(ii) *Linotype*

The linotype machine incorporates both the keyboard and caster within one frame and both the operations are controlled by one operator. It stores its type characters in a large number of single matrices in the magazine of the machine. A monotype caster uses only one matrix for each individual character, linotype carries a number of identical matrices for each character. As a result of this a complete line is composed as one piece instead of casting each character individually.

Linotype was invented in 1886 by Ottmar Mergenthaler of Baltimore. Intertype which is also based on linotype principle was developed in 1911. Because both these machines cast lines of type (called slug), they are also called slug casting machines.

The system works like this: The keyboard operator adjusts the machine to set type to a desired pica measure and leading. When the operator presses a key on the keyboard, this causes the appropriate matrix to drop from the magazine to an assembly point above the keyboard. The operator presses the key buttons one after another till a line is completed in a given width. The assembled line of matrices is now transferred to a type moulding unit which casts the metal line of types (slug) and then transfers the cast line in the galley and distributes the brass matrices in the respective boxes for further composing and casting purpose.

The linotype machine can set in a large variety of type faces ranging from 4¾ point to 48 points. Some condensed typefaces can be set upto 60 point. The machines are used mainly in the newspaper industry where they are employed for composing type of standard size in variable column setting.

Standard line casting machine is designed to set type from one magazine at a time. This magazine contains 90 duplex (double characters) mats, capable of setting either two styles of the same type face or two different type faces. There are innovative models that set type from two different magazines at one time. This makes possible mixing of four type styles such as roman, italic, roman bold and italic bold. Models with two or four magazines allow speedy change over of magazine for design.

(iii) *Intertype,*

Intertype machines are much faster in work but not free from certain pitfalls. Corrections are more difficult to perform. For a single correction the entire line or even all succeeding lines in the paragraph may be required to be reset. The characters on the slug can not be altered in any way as the whole line is one piece of metal. Problems also arise from wear of the matrices. If they do not fit snugly together, excess metal can be forced up between them to print as fine hairlines between letters. Tiny pieces of grit between the matrices can also cause the same problem.

(iv) *Ludlow Caster*

Ludlow is a proprietary name of a display size type casting machine which uses hand assembled matrices. The ludlow system is a combination of hand composing and line composing; The system was conceived by Washington Ludlow and. later perfected by A. Reade in 1906. The first Ludlow machine appeared in 1911 and was an advancement in hot metal Composing.

Ludlow system can be defined as a semi mechanical line casting machine mainly used for display work. The system consists of (i) a composing stick, (ii) matrices, (iii) cabinets, and (iv) a casting machine. Brass matrices are set justified by hand in a composing stick and locked in it. The stick full of matrices is inserted in the Ludlow typographic casting machine and a knob is pressed. Depression of the lever moves the machine whereby, the type slug comes out in the galley. The stick is taken out of the casting machine. A proof is pulled out after which the slug is melted down for reuse.

The Ludlow system was developed for display type composition and can produce letters upto 144 point and figures upto 240 point. The system had certain advantages over hand composing as Ludlow type is always new and free from defects of using a worn out type.

## COLD COMPOSING

Cold composing can be explained as a method of composing which does not use hot metal for casting type for printing. Cold composing is also known as phototypesetting. Increasing cost of type metal has made phototypesetting an important alternative to mechanical hot metal composing.

Speed is a distinct advantage of phototypesetting system due to reduction of mechanical movements. Phototypesetting provides fast, flexible, clean and relatively inexpensive method of setting type through photographic means on photo sensitive film or paper which can be directly used for making off-set plates for final printing. Cold composing is also called flat type composing, and non-metallic composing.

Photocomposing or cold composing can be divided into the following three categories:

1. Photomechanical
2. Digital Cathod Ray Tube (CRT)
3. Laser composing

### *Photomechanical*

In photomechanical method images are produced by shining of light through a glass or film negative of the character onto a photographic film or paper. There are two main categories of cold type photomechanical composing:

1. Electric Typewriter Composing
2. Phototypesetting System

*Electric Typewriter Composing*

Electric typewriter system consists of two units. The keyboard unit and the caster unit. The keyboard unit receives, corrects, changes, shuffles and memorises the instructions given by the operator. Electric typewriter keyboard with some modifications types the copy. The typed image is converted into the requisite; printing image carrier by means of photography and photo-mechanics.

In electric typewriter composing, the reproduction copy from which off-set printing plates will be made is created by exposing photo-sensitive paper or film where light formed into shapes of type characters one by one. The paper or film is processed like any other photograph under safe light. In this system copy is directly typed on to repro paper, either manually or automatically. Corrections are inexpensive.

The typewriter composing also has its limitations. It produces only one repro. If more than one is required either the job has to be retyped or the tape has to be run through again to produce a second copy.

*Phototypesetting System*

Phototypesetting is a fast and inexpensive method of setting type through photographic means. Phototypesetting mechanism is guided by four characteristics.

1. Character storage with photographic negative/positive on film or light sensitive paper is the common feature of phototypesetting. Character storage enables to view on the screen electronically. In advance mechanics, the characters are stored in magnetic diskettes and cassettes.
2. Controlled light source so that the density of type matter remains the same throughout the whole page.
3. Enlargement or reduction of image area with the help of lenses possible.
4. Positioning of characters to set the next character adjacent to the earlier exposed one in a position so that words and characters may maintain legibility and readability. This also helps controlling space between lines.

Phototypesetting has the following advantages:

(i) Type is sharper and there is no pressure of metal type against the paper which may cause ink squeeze and tend to make edges of the printed matter irregular.

(ii) It is easier to acquire accuracy in type size and inter-linear spacing.

(iii) In phototypesetting, since no metal is used, letters can be set touching, over lapping and in any other way one wishes to display.

(iv) Changing type faces is easy and simple.

(v) Page make up can be done on visual display screen of the phototypesetting machine. Positioning of illustrations, captions, headings etc. can be changed with ease.

## CATHODE RAY TUBE (CRT)

Cathode Ray Tube is a vacuum tube, such as television picture tube or a computer system display device, which is used to show images of data or design. It is especially useful in settings where information often needs to be modified or rearranged.

In a Cathode Ray Tube advanced computer electronics and electronic video tube is used for producing character image either by a contact process where a film or paper is placed over the front of the cathode ray tube or by optical transmission of the tube beamed directly on to the film or paper. It is much more faster than ordinary photocomposing machine.

The main features of the CRT system are (i) formation and (ii) projection. Formation means computer logic character formation. In this system characters are stored as digital information in the computer. The computer will flash the set of characters to the Cathode Ray Tube as electronic signals when commanded.

Lens in the machine helps in focussing and projecting the needed information to form each character on photosensitive film or paper as series of dots.

Some machines use formation for projecting the information on to the photosensitive film or paper. In this character projection is done by scanning the character to be set that translates this information by breaking it down to thousands of lines. These lines are transmitted to Cathode Ray Tube and projected on to the photosensitive film or paper.

This makes possible to complete page make up with both text and illustration. Page making can be done on photosensitive (bromide) paper, film or even offset plates.

CRT system has certain advantages over other phototypesetting systems. It can set type in ½ point increments and spacing between two lines can be 0.1 point *i.e.* 1/10th part of a point. Because of very high speed in composing, CRTs are mainly used for newspapers, books, periodicals, telephone directories where high speed composing is required.

## LASER

In this method of composing LASER instead of CRT is used to produce the image. Light Amplification by Stimulated Emission of Radiation (LASER) is a light beam of specific kind which can apply vast energy by extreme accuracy. A laser system comprises of three main elements *viz.* (i) an amplifying medium, (ii) a resonator, and (iii) a power supply.

The laser is used to project an extremely small accurate spot of light directly onto the photographic film or paper, creating a sharp dense image of the character. The machine uses the laser as the light source to digitise characters. The digitised fonts are translated into a form understood by the computer system and are stored on magnetic cartridge or discs. This technology is used in the photocomposing machines. It is one of the fastest method of setting the matter through photographic means.

# 13

# Desk Top Publishing

Desk Top Publishing is the use of a personal computer to perform publishing tasks that would otherwise require much more complicated equipment and human effort. Desktop publishing allows an individual to combine text, numerical data, photographs, charts, and other visual elements in a document that can be printed on a laser printer or more advanced typesetting machine. The primary advantages of desktop publishing over conventional publishing apparatus are low cost and ease of use.

A typical desktop publishing system comprises a personal computer, a video monitor, a high-resolution printer, and various input devices, such as a keyboard, mouse, or digital scanner. Some systems also integrate advanced memory storage units, communication devices, and other peripheral equipment. One or a number of different combinations of software applications is necessary to operate the system. Text and graphic elements are commonly created or manipulated with several separate software programs and then combined with, or copied into, a page-makeup program that allows the user to arrange them into a final composite. More powerful desktop publishing software programs offer full-featured word processing and graphics capabilities.

Desk Top Publishing (DTP) is the power of personal computer to create paper based publication that until very recently required powerful machines and highly skilled craftsmen to produce. It is a medium of producing screen based, camera ready copy and artwork without recourse to conventional cut and paste system.

Desk Top Publishing is the result of developments in three other technologies.

1. Graphically based personal computers
2. Low cost laser printer

3. New computer language specifically intended to describe entire page at once.

But it was not until 1984 when Apple Macintosh introduced the magic of DTP system that anyone could use. Coupled with the developments in other computer languages and laser printers which could produce a variety of type styles in an infinite variety of sizes. This made possible for a Macintosh user to produce phototypeset pages from a desk top literally. Introduction of Page Maker technology changed the way of producing a printed page.

*How DTP works*

DTP is usually understood as a publishing process, whereas it is primarily a system of composing pages. When the text is fed into the computer, it comes on the monitor screen. It is possible to play about with the format, the way it should look on the page, shift the graphics and photographs till you get a page that is exactly the way you want it to be.

The main features of DTP are:

1. It is able to use multiple type fonts in a single document or page.
2. It can combine text and graphic in a single computer printed document.
3. It can create page layout or place previously created text and graphics into that layout.
4. It has the ability to see in part or all of a page as it will print and modify the page until it has achieved the desired appearance.
5. It can format a page by deciding or altering columns, margins, gutters etc.

The DIP system to work needs a *Personal Computer* which serves as the data entry device in which text and graphics are transferred from other sources, typing directly on the keyboard or via scanners and digitisers.

Another device essential to operate a DTP system is a *Laser printer* for producing reproduction of the data fed into the computer directly on a plain paper. It allows the printing of text and graphics simultaneously.

The *Computer Programme* allows finalisation of page layout with cut and paste on the computer screen with the help of softwares.

## PAGE MAKER AND DTP

There are many page composition softwares available but most commonly used in DTP is the Page Maker. Page Maker is a page composition software package which gives all your printed pages or documents a neat and professional look.

Page Maker makes it possible to work upto five different views of a page and it is possible to work on two facing pages side by side. It is possible to manipulate general characteristics like page size, margins, columns etc. One can import graphics from other sources and introduce variety in typographical presentation on a single page. It is possible to move, resize and vertically resize the text block.

Other main features of the Page Maker include, editing of text by correcting errors of spellings, deleting certain portions and adding a few lines or paragraphs instead.

The programme contains certain graphics such as charts, graphs, borders, boxes, circles etc. which can be used to highlight the text.

All the pages in the text can be numbered automatically and any alteration is also possible without disturbing any arrangement.

### *Advantages and Disadvantages*

Desk Top Publishing has revolutionized the composing scene. It is much more economical, efficient and quick in production and has unmatched quality control with the ability to not only edit but allows author's alterations without taking much time and money. It ensures complete control over contents and aesthetics.

The processes of pulling out galleys, paste up, proof marking and carrying corrections have been eliminated by this system.

The system also has its pitfalls with some traditional fonts with thick and thin strokes and differing character width and other complex fonts, the output is not very attractive.

The ability to use multiple typefaces in one page layout by this system, if put to use makes distracting reading.

# 14

# New Technologies

New technological developments have affected the publishing scene the world over. The electronic edge has added new dimensions to publishing and printing. The computer, the word processor and all the sophisticated devices and accessories such as Desk Top publishing, Windows, etc. inspire and challenge the publishing scene today.

*The reprography revolution* initiated the photo reproduction technology also posed challenges to copyright. It permitted individual reader to easily make copies of printed materials. Publishers also exploited this successfully. By 1970s the advent of new technology made transmission, storage and distribution of data easy and within reach of a common man.

*The internet* developed in 1970s as an experimental network designed to support military research which enables messages, text and visuals to be sent on one host on one network to any host on another, has revolutionized the information and communication technology. Internet has been hailed by the world publishing fraternity as a welcome friend in the international expansion of publishing. As the reading devices became more compact and sophisticated, several of the largest US publishing houses opened on line publishing ventures. Internet has proved to be a major ally of publishing industry with online firms like Amazone.com boosting sales of conventional books at heavily discounted prices to the 'surfing shoppers' reaching for their screens on their personal PCs. Internet book sales account has already touched 15% of the total book sale in the United States. In Asia alone it is estimated that the number of internet users is expected to reach 228 million by the end of this decade.

*E-Book* is another development of the electronic edge, which gave 'electronic book'. E-book combines the storage, search capabilities and adaptability of a traditional book. Thousands of books have been digitized, to be read on line, downloaded, printed by the readers; thus assuring that their electronic version need never go out of print.

An eBook is an *electronic* version of a traditional print book that can be read by using a personal computer or by using an eBook reader. One can purchase an eBook on diskette or CD, but the most popular method of getting an eBook is to purchase a downloadable file of the eBook (or other reading material) from a Web site to be read from one's own computer or reading device. An eBook can be downloaded quickly.

Although it is not necessary to use a reader application or device in order to read an eBook (most books can be read as PDFfiles), they are popular because they enable options similar to those of a paper book - readers can bookmark pages, make notes, highlight passages, and save selected text. In addition to these familiar possibilities, eBook readers also include built-in dictionaries, and alterable font sizes and styles.

Typically, an eBook reader ia a light weight, hand-held device and can store from four thousand to over half a million pages of text and graphics. A popular feature is its back-lit screen which makes reading in the dark possible.

Some eBooks can be downloaded for free or at reduced cost, however, prices for many eBooks—especially bestsellers—are similar to those of hardcover books, and are sometimes higher. Most eBooks at Barnes and Noble, for example, are comparable in price to their traditional print versions.

PDF (Portable Document Format) is a file format that has captured all the elements of a printed document as an electronic image that you can view, navigate, print, or forward to someone else. PDF files are created using Adobe Acrobat, Acrobat Capture, or similar products. To view and use the files, you need the free Acrobat Reader, which you can easily download. Once you've downloaded the Reader, it will start automatically whenever you want to look at a PDF file.

PDF files are especially useful for documents such as magazine articles, product brochures, or flyers in which you want to preserve the original graphic appearance online. A PDF file contains one or more page images, each of which you can zoom in on or out from. You can page forward and backward.

PDF files are useful in the development of graphic design where members of the design team are working at different places. It is also useful for online distribution of printed documented where you can provide the printed appearance

Acrobat's PDF files are more than images of documents. Files can embed type fonts so that they're available at any viewing location. They can also include interactive elements such as buttons for forms entry etc..

*Print on demand (POD)* is a publishing business model. The main distinguishing mark for print (or publish) on demand is that a copy is not created until an order is received. Print on demand with digital technology is used as a way of publishing book to order for a fixed cost per copy, irrespective of the size of the order. Digital technology is ideally suited to publish small print runs of books and posters (often as a single copy) as and when they are needed. While the unit price of each physical book printed is higher than with offset printing, when setup costs are taken into account. Digital print on demand provides a lower per unit costs for a very small print runs than traditional printing methods.

While the unit cost of a book or a print produced on POD is usually higher than the one produced as part of a larger print run, POD does bring some key business benefits: (1) Large inventories of book need not be kept in stock. (2) The technical set-up is quicker and less expansive than the traditional printing. (3) There is little or no waste from unsold products. These advantages reduce the risks associated with publishing books.

*Project Gutenberg* was started in 1971 when one Michael Hart was given millions of dollars worth computer time by the operators of the Xerox sigma V at the Materials Research Lab at the university of Illinois. He thought that the greatest value created by computers would be the storage, retrieval, and searching of what was stored in our libraries.

He proceeded to type in the "Declaration of Independence" and tried to send it to everyone on the networks.

The premise on which Michael Hart based Project Gutenberg was: anything that can be entered into a computer can be reproduced indefinitely. He called it 'Replicator Technology'. The concept of replicator technology is simple; once a book or any other item (including pictures, sounds, and even 3-D items can be stored in a computer), then any number of copies can and will be available. Every one in the world can have a copy of a book that has been entered into a computer.

Project Gutenberg has almost completed 10,000 books in Project Gutenberg Electronic Library. There are three portions of the Project Gutenberg library:

Light literature; such as Alice in wonderland, Peter Pan, etc.

Heavy literature; such as the Bible or other religious documents. Shakespeare, Moby Dick, Paradise Lost, etc.

References; such as Roget's Thesaurus, almanacs, and encyclopedias, dictionaries, etc.

Project Gutenberg was part of celebrations of the 100th Anniversary of Public libraries, starting in 1995 in America.

# 15

# Printing Processes

It is important for a production manager to decide the process of printing according to the size of the job. The selection of printer and process of printing would largely depend upon the publisher's capacity to pay for the process and the requirements of the book to be printed.

The factors which one should keep in mind while deciding the process of printing would include the size of the edition, the amount of funds earmarked for the printing of the book, capacity of the printer to print according to the standards required, the time available for completion of the job and the type of paper required to be used for your kind of book.

Different processes have their unique advantages and disadvantages. The printing industry has undergone tremendous change during the past one decade. The advent of computer and desk top publishing has revolutionised the process of book making.

Nevertheless, for printing of books the four most commonly used processes are discussed in the following pages. These are:

1. Letterpress
2. Offset
3. Intaglio
4. Screen Printing

Production manager would match the process of printing with his needs and suggest the same for the book in hand.

## LETTERPRESS PRINTING

Letterpress printing can be defined as a process by which images are transferred by pressure from an inked surface on to a paper. Letterpress printing requires a relief printing surface. It means that a surface in which the parts that are to print are raised above the level of the parts that are not to be printed. In a printing type, therefore, the image of the letter is raised above the surface of the type body. This method of printing is popularly known as *relief printing* or printing by letterpress.

The basis of letterpress is the process that Gutenberg invented in 1454 by using movable type—metal type which can be rearranged or recomposed and could become printing surface which can be used and reused several times. This invention became a landmark in human history, making the beginning of large scale printing in Europe and later in the rest of the world.

Prior to movable metal type the books were printed by woodcut, employing the same principle of relief printing where impression can be made after inking the raised surface and pressing it against the paper.

The direct physical contact between the printing surface and the paper gives sharpness, crispness and controlled impression to the letterpress process of printing. Inspite of high technological advances in the field of letterpress printing, the underlying principles of the letterpress remain the same *i.e.* inking the raised surface, positioning the paper, making an impression and delivery, of the printed sheet. Since the process is mechanical, the good results depend upon the following factors:

1. Efficiency of the components of the press
2. Skill of the operator
3. Nature of printing surface.

*Registering*

Positioning of type and blocks correctly is known as registering. It can be defined as accurate positioning of printing on a page or adjustment of the printing surface so that it may print the matter in correct position. This is done to ensure that each page image will exactly back up the page image on the other side of a sheet. Registering is necessary to ensure that printed lines of one side of the page falls exactly on the printed lines of its back. It is exact adjustment in back to back printing.

Registering is to print an impression on a sheet in correct relationship to other impressions already printed on the same sheet. In case of illustration using three or four colour plates, each will have to be printed exactly in position so that there is no overlapping otherwise, the printing will not form the composite image. When such impressions are not exact it is called *out of register.*

*Makeready*

In simple terms makeready is setting up a printing machine ready to run specific job. It includes such matters as pressure and alignment, evenness of the raised printing surface, adjustments, ink changes and placing of plates on the press. Though the surfaces of types and forme bed are flat but no form or block, however, competently composed or engraved is ever perfect. The fact that letters of varying width exert varying pressure on impact certain adjustment to compensate for evenness is necessary.

The process of preparing a forme and correcting unevenness so that the final impression is clear and distinct and that there are no uneven impressions which are either too heavy or too light is called makeready. It may also mean all adjustments preliminary to printing a specific job on a specific quality of paper.

The first printed sheet will reveal that some of the letters are printing heavily while others are printing lightly. Therefore, the lighter portions must be made heavier and heavier portions must be made lighter to give an even look to the printed matter.

Evenness of impression is achieved by the following three types:

1. Pasting of pieces of paper under type, rules or block that are lower than the rest of the type in the forme. This is called underlaying.
2. If there is a gap between a plate and its mount a specially prepared a cutsheet is interlayed to increase or decrease the pressure.
3. Sometimes pieces of paper are overlayed on the tympan or cylinder to give more pressure or parts are cut away from tympan or cylinder to reduce the pressure.

The quality printing by letterpress demands that plane of the whole printing press is absolutely even. The process consumes a lot of time and economy or haste in this way mean less than desired quality of job. Because the quality of printing depends largely on the time spent in *makeready*.

*Striking*

After the makeready stage is over and the forme has been placed in an absolutely even state, the forme is laid flat on the bed of the machine known in the printing parlance as 'putting to bed'. The matter is then printed by applying ink on the type. The paper is fed either by hand or by machine depending upon the kind of letterpress. Printing image is transferred by making the inked surface contact with the paper. This is why letterpress process of printing is also known as 'direct contact process'.

Letterpress printing machines are of the following four types:

(i) Platen press
(ii) Cylinder press
(iii) Rotary press
(iv) Belt press

(i) *Platen Press*

It is the simplest form of the letterpress printing. In this process flat surfaces of the assembled forme and sheet of paper are brought together vertically under pressure to create an impression. The flat surface where sheet of paper is placed is called 'platen'. When the platen closes the paper comes in direct contact with inked type bed and the impact results in an impression on the paper. In some kinds of presses the platen moves to make contact with the forme, while in others the forme moves to make contact with the platen.

Special features of the platen press are the rotating disc, inking rollers and a direct roller. When the paper is fed in these machines by hand these are called 'handfed machines'. These days most of machines are fed automatically. The speed of printing in this. process is low, though it prints efficiently in the smaller sizes and in single colour.

Platen machines usually print a foolscape size of paper, most platen can handle larger high class work, mainly using automatic colour register system.

(ii) *Cylinder Press*

In a cylinder press impression is obtained by means of revolving cylinder which carries a sheet of paper and presses it against the face of the forme, which is maintained in a flat horizontal bed reciprocating below the cylinder.

Cylinder presses also print from flat forms and plates. This is a high speed process and thousands of copies can be obtained in one hour. In this process the type or plates are held on a horizontal or vertical plane (bed) while ink rollers and sheet of paper, carried by a cylinder, alternately pass over it. Horizontal beds are called flat beds.

The principle of cylinder press can be explained as follows:

1. The flat bed moves forward under ink rollers and touches the paper as it passes beneath the impression cylinder.
2. The impression is transferred, but the cylinder continues to revolve as the bed stops and starts coming back.
3. The cylinder rises slightly to allow the bed to pass under it and in the same action delivers the printed sheet.
4. The cylinder picks up the other sheet as the bed starts forward again under the ink rollers.

The cycle is repeated with high speed and printed sheets are passed on to the delivery end.

Cylinder presses are capable of handling bigger sheet sizes. These machines are sheet fed and their speed depends upon the efficiency with which the paper is fed on to the cylinder. The press can print a single impression for each pass of the machine bed. An improvement in the cylinder machine is called perfecting machine which can print both sides of the sheet.

(iii) *Rotary Press*

Rotary press is an advancement on the cylinder press. Rotary press carries curved printing plates set into a rotating cylinder with the surface to be printed. In this process of printing, movable type is not used. Instead, curved plates and stereos, plastic or rubber plates or newly developed photopolymer plates are clamped on the cylinders. The cylinders carry the plates and rotate continuously, inking being carried out by rollers in contact with the plates.

A rotary press which prints from individual sheets of paper is called sheet fed press. When continuous roll (web) of paper is used for printing, it is called web fed rotary. In a web fed rotary system the back of the paper is printed on a separate pair of cylinders. In this process the paper is taken to first pair of cylinders and printed on one side then taken to second pair of cylinders and printed on the reverse side. The paper is fed from a reel and passes in a strip through the machine where it is cut into sheets and folded into signatures before the web reaches the delivery end.

The printing industry has undergone a tremendous change. Today the computer, laser technology and video screen are taking over the many functions of the printing press. But the web fed rotary is still one of the fastest printing process in terms of impressions per hour.

(iv) *Belt Press*

It is a bookwork press which binds the book as it prints. The belt press is generally known by the trade name of its inventor *Cameron.* The cameron belt press operates on different principle. In this system a number of flexible plates are assembled not around a printing cylinder, but on two wide continuous belts which come into contact with the web of paper. These flexible plates are made of plastic or photopolymer and are produced either from a mould made from a forme or photographically.

One of these two flexible continuous belts which are mounted on the machine, one belt contains one half of the plates, the other half of the plates is mounted on the other belt. These belts are of variable length to accommodate wide ranges of extent. The paper roll passes first over one belt of pages and is turned to be printed over the second belt. The web passes through a number of ribbons and the process can print, cut into pages, gather sections and collate them into books.

An adhesive line can be attached and in combination with the belt press it can print and bind a voluminous book in one go. This printing cum binding machine is very useful for the printing of paperbacks.

*Advantages of Letter press*

1. New jobs with smaller print run are cheaper to produce.
2. It is easier to make last minute changes and adjustments in the composed matter.
3. Direct physical contact between printing surface and paper gives sharp, crisp and controlled impression.

*Disadvantages*

1. It takes more time for 'make ready'.

2. Printing of fine halftone illustration needs high quality paper.
3. Speed of printing is comparatively lower in sheetfed machine.
4. Most letter presses print one colour at a time. Thus multicolour printing becomes a time consuming job.
5. In multicolour printing, registering is done every time and any inaccuracy may spoil the printing quality.
6. Uneven pressure or slight variation in it may result in indention and hamper readability of the printed matter.
7. Cost of producing plates is high.

## OFFSET PRINTING, PLANOGRAPHIC PRINTING (LITHOGRAPHY)

In planographic printing process the print is made from a plane or flat surface in contrast to other major contact printing methods which print from raised surface (as in letter press) as described above or incised surface (as in Gravure) described in the following pages. The process is also known as lithography, offset printing, offset lithography or photo offset. This is the major form of planographic printing in use throughout the world for books and periodicals.

Uptill the beginning of 20th century Stone (Litho) was used for the purpose but with the introduction of new technologies, stone plates have been replaced by metal treated plates. The process of lithography printing works on the principle that grease and water do not mix. In this process printing is done on plates in which printing areas are made grease receptive and non-print areas are made water receptive.

The principle works like this:

1. The surface of the plate is processed into flat grease receptive and water receptive areas. Grease receptive areas are printing areas and water receptive areas are non-printing areas.
2. The wetting or dampening of the surface plate.
3. Spreading of greasy ink so that the non printing dampen areas would repel greasy ink.
4. Paper is placed against the plate to transfer the printing areas on the paper.

In offset process, during printing the printing image is transferred from the plate to the blanket and thereafter from blanket to the paper so that less water comes in contact with the paper. Since the paper does not come in direct contact with the printing plate the process is also called indirect method of printing.

*Advantages*

1. Offset method of printing is cost effective, cheaper and faster for jobs with larger print runs.
2. The process is most useful for printing of textbooks which require frequent reprinting.
   Offset machines can be divided into three categories.
   (i) Small offset—These are small machines which can print single colour single side on a particular size of the sheet.
   (ii) Sheetfed offset. These are single colour single side machines and single colour perfectors which can print on both sides. Multicolour machines are also available. These machines can print on sheets variant in size.
   (iii) Web offset. These machines are for high run colour printing which also fold the roll while they print. Such machines can provide folded sections ready for gathering and binding.
3. Economy of storage space is an added advantage. Offset plates require very little space and negatives from which the plates are made can be revised if another printing is required.
4. Technological advances have provided greater economy in typography. Direct printing from typing by word processor and other computer printouts has been made possible in this process.
5. It is possible to achieve soft gradation in offset printing which is unthinkable in letterpress printing.
6. Printing of complex artwork which may cost a lot of money if produced on letterpress can be economically produced on offset without incurring extra expenses.
7. Multicolour printing can also be done at much faster speed.
8. Recomposing the matter for reprinting job is eliminated as the reprinting can be directly done from the plates.
9. For printing of illustrations and drawings no separate plates/blocks or paper is required.

*Disadvantages*

1. The result of printing is not that sharp and crisp as in the letterpress.

2. Corrections and changes are a cumbersome process as it involves the preparation of the plate again.
3. Even and uniform impression is difficult to achieve in small print runs.
4. Since the process is based upon ink spread and water flow, the proper balance, sometimes becomes difficult to maintain.

## INTAGLIO OR GRAVURE PRINTING

Gravure is an intaglio printing in which printing surface is recessed. Unlike letterpress where the printing surface is raised or specially treated smooth surface as in offset, intaglio or Gravure process of printing surface has depressions which hold the ink. As the image has been etched below the surface of the plate, when plate is inked, the ink flows into cuts. The excess ink is removed off the surface of the plate with the help of a thin blade called 'doctor blade'. The ink remaining in the cuts or cells prints on paper in contact with the plate. When the process is done as a rotary press it is called *Rotogravure.*

In making the gravure plate, photographic negatives and positives are carefully printed first without a screen and then after all the elements have been mounted into position through an overall grid which regulates the amount of ink in the cells created by the screen. Light is passed through the positive to a sensitised carbon sheet which is fastened to the plate developed and etched.

In photogravure the image is printed in ink held in small recesses or pits in a copper faced steel cylinder. The process is suitable for very wide range of work but is mostly used for printing of periodicals. The process is useful for printing bigger print runs because the initial cost of making the printing surface is very high since all the printing elements are screened on the printing surface.

The thick dense body of ink gives richness to the impression. The fact that the ink is wiped out off the plate on each impression, a thin, fast drying ink is required to be used for best results. The minutest and most complicated design can be printed with utmost clarity. Gravure method of printing can give smoothness to the tiniest of scratch on the surface. The intaglio line engraving is, therefore, more prominent and distinct than achieved through relief process of printing. This process can give better results in terms of depth of colour, delicacy and brightness of lighter tones. The process is best suitable for reproducing photographs. Pictures can be printed on a relatively cheap paper.

## SCREEN PRINTING

Screen printing is the simplest of all forms of printings. The principle of screen printing is said to have been based upon the old Chinese method of stencilling. This process is in wide variety of uses since the beginning of the 20th century. The process was earlier known as silk screen printing as the screen used for filtering the image was silk. These days screens are made of nylon, linen and metal wire.

The process of silk screen printing is very simple. The screen fabric is stretched over a wooden frame. The stencil of the image to be printed is attached to the screen which now serves as the image carrier. The stencil is made on the screen by using photographic material. The frame is hinged to the table firmly. The paper or article to be printed, is placed below the frame on the table top. Ink is forced through the screen and the stencil by a flat piece of rubber called 'squeezee'. The ink filters through the printing and non-printing areas of the screen image on the printing surface placed below. The process of forcing the ink through the stencil is done by hand or by automatic machines.

Screens are available in different sizes depending upon the size of the matter to be printed. Materials used in this process are fewer in number and simpler in operation. It requires a wooden frame to hold the screen, a hinged table to hold the frame, ink and Squeezee. The stencil is made of photographic material.

Screen printing has variety of applications from labelling on glass or plastic bottles to printing circuits on electronic equipments. Screen printing can be achieved on surfaces which are not flat even curved and circular surfaces can also be printed with utmost clarity and ease. Development of new technologies and machines has made an otherwise slow process, a fast printing method for quality jobs.

# 16

# Proof Reading

Proof reading is an integral part of the printing process. The process of book production is a combination of certain sequences which include designing, casting off, selection of process of printing, composing the matter in type and correcting the matter thus composed before starting the print run.

Proof reading plays an important role in producing good quality books. A book full of printing errors discourages the reader and lowers its interest in the publication and can turn an otherwise important work as worthless and frustrating experience by a reader.

New advances in printing technology have revolutionised the methods of book production. Proof reading terms, methods of marking the proofs have remained almost unchanged. A thorough knowledge of these is still a major force in producing good books.

## PROOF DEFINED

A proof is a trial print or sheet of any printed material made before the production run, that is checked against the original manuscript and upon which corrections are marked. These are test images of composed matter drawn from that matter at any of several stages of printing process as from galleys, composed pages etc.

A proof may also be described as a trial pull from type matter or from plates to show the state of the work, and for checking and correcting if necessary. A series of later proofs taken after corrections have been carried out are called 'revises'.

## TYPES OF PROOFS

The following types of proofs are required at different stages of book production.

### *Galley proofs*

A galley is a metal tray usually of a size to hold three pages of octavo size. The type arranged in the galley is called matter. Proofs drawn from such types of trays set in single column of any width are known as galley proofs. These are the first uncorrected proofs prior to page make up. In hot metal composing, galley proofs are taken from the tray or galley of type after it leaves the casting machine. These proofs come in a long narrow strip of paper.

When the galley tray is filled with lines of composed matter in a required line measure the galley proof is taken out. The machine used for pulling out proofs from galleys is called 'proof press' or 'galley press'. These presses are manually operated as well as automatic.

The proofs are taken out by placing the galley on the bed of the press with composed matter firmly held. An ink roller called *brayer* is passed over the type. A sheet of paper is placed on the inked type and another roller called impression cylinder is passed over the paper. The pressure transfers the ink from type to the paper.

Galley proofs contain all the compositor's errors, mistakes of the author and keyboard operator depending upon the method used in composing the matter. Only a careful observation of the galley proofs will enable the proof reader to detect deviation from the original. Attention at this stage needs to be paid to figures, punctuation, spelling mistakes, dropped words, broken type, repeated lines etc.

These proofs are usually read by proofreader and author and errors are corrected by compositor while the type remains in this form. These are un made up text taken out for marking corrections before pages are made out of the composed. matter into the required size. When corrections are heavy, revised galleys are taken out.

### *Revised galley proofs*

These are proofs taken again on galleys after the corrections have been carried out from the first galley proofs. Revised galley proofs form the basis for breaking the composed matter into required size of pages. Addition and deletion of matter at this stage is possible and less cumbersome than changes in matter after the pages have been cast out of galleys.

*Pages on galley proofs*

These proofs are still on galleys. Pages on galley proofs have the text matter broken up into pages after the corrections have been carried out from galleys or revised galleys. These proofs are taken out of galley length paper with three or four pages on each sheet of proof. Upto this stage the composed matter is still in the galleys with pieces of furniture separating the made up pages.

These proofs are taken out sometimes before the regular page proofs by breaking the type in the galleys into required number of lines per page. The break up of the composed matter into page length includes the running heads and other elements of each individual page.

*Page proofs*

These are set proofs of fully composed matter and laid out pages assembled for a final checking operation before the book is printed. These proofs are taken out after the corrections have been carried out on galleys or pages on galleys. Some publishers straightway get the matter composed into pages bypassing the galley stage. These are sometimes called *book proofs.*

Unless directly composed as pages, page proofs are made up by breaking the galleys of type into required number of lines per page. Page proofs also include running heads, titles, illustrations, page numbers etc. in their appropriate position.

Page proofs are required to be checked thoroughly since elements of page layout like running heads, folios, page length etc. appear for the first time in proofs after galleys. Page proofs also give an idea of the layout of the book and arrangement of the text matter.

Unlike galleys, page proofs provide very little scope for addition or deletion in the text matter. Changes at this stage would not only disturb the printing schedule but also increase the cost of composing—the two things which should always be kept under control by the production manager.

*Lithographic proofs*

In hot metal composing, where matter is composed on hot metal machine, proofs are read and corrections are marked as described above for proofs on letter press. It is only after the proofs have been marked and corrections carried out that the photographic plates are made for reproduction pull outs. Corrections on photographic proofs are marked in the same manner as galleys or page proofs. The corrections are carried out by the operator by cutting out the incorrect word or line from the original sheet of film setting and inserting the corrected word or line in that place.

*Repro proofs*

A camera ready copy or proof of material to be printed is called repro proof or repro. From metal type, repros are printed on special coated paper. Printer's negatives are made from camera ready copies for making printing plates.

In hot metal composing, repro proofs are taken in the form of high quality ink impression on a dull coated paper. Perfect impression is achieved by repro proofs which in turn, enables good quality printing possible.

Corrections in repro proofs are made by patching and pasting a wrong word or line with a corrected one at the appropriate place. To do this job, two sets of repro proofs should be available. Sometimes corrections are marked with light blue pencil in the margin so that correction marks are not picked up by the camera after these are carried out.

*Foundry proofs*

In letter press printing, proofs drawn from a forme ready for the press, before actual printing begins, are called foundry proofs. In other words, proofs or pages locked up in a chase are called foundry proofs. When all corrections having been completed and the job being passed on for press, a final pull is made of type matter before being passed to the foundry for casting.

*Machine proofs*

Last to come in the series of proofs are the machine proofs. These are taken by the machine minder immediately before starting the printing of formes. These are usually read by the printer's men because this is the last opportunity to realise the previously undetected mistakes. These proofs are not meant to be sent to the author or editor as this would mean holding up the machine.

In other words when formes are on the machine and make ready the machine mender usually uses first few copies as machine proofs to have a final look at the composed matter in terms of positioning and inking before starting the print run.

Machine proofs serve a useful purpose in printing halftones and colour work. If halftones are murky, patchy and containing small bits of white spots or on the contrary giving a poor contrast or in case of colour work not registering properly and positioning of colours is not in order, the last minute adjustments are made by seeing the machine proofs before starting the print run. These proofs help to see whether everyline on the page is exactly over the corresponding line on the reverse side of the page so that it does not hinder readability.

Machine proofs are the last stage where any change, alteration, correction can be made. Machine proofs help visualising the correct imposition of pages, the proper spread of ink on paper etc.

## OTHER RELATED CONCEPTS

There are some other related concepts which deserve special mentioning. These are:

(i) *First proof:* This is a term used to denote first set of proofs taken by the printer for marking corrections. These may be in galleys or made up pages.

(ii) *Master proof:* When two sets of proofs are sent to the author by the publisher for making corrections, the one on which corrections are marked and sent back for carrying out corrections is called master proof. Sometimes more than one set of proofs is sent by the printer and the set on which all corrections are transferred and sent to the printer for carrying out mistakes is also called master proof.

*Final proof:* It is the set of proofs which are finalised as ready for printing. Actually these are page proofs where the author or the editor puts his/her signatures as a signal to the printer to go ahead for printing the pages. After the corrections, if any, in the final proofs are carried out, the forme is 'make ready' for final print run and machine minder takes out the machine proofs (discussed above) for the last look before starting the printing of the forme.

*Author's Alterations:* These are changes or alterations in the copy introduced at proof stage as distinct from the errors of composing. Alterations or additions made by an author other than the printer's errors in the composed matter are known as author's alterations (AA's).

These changes mean departure from the original copy. The printer is only responsible for setting an easily legible copy correctly, following general instructions regarding page layout and printing the matter thus composed in a manner which is acceptable as good standard of printing.

Such changes are usually suggested by authors when they see the galleys. Some authors go the extent of suggesting changes in the manuscript when the pages have been composed. These alterations do not only relate to basic text, sometimes headings, illustrations and design also become items of alterations.

An average author does not realise that corrections are reckoned by printers as piece work and charged by time and since these are fiddling jobs which take disproportionately long time and that the time spent on them depends upon the efficiency and industry of individual workman and that consequently the cost of corrections can easily amount up to a considerable sum.

Alterations at this stage mean forme has to come off the machine, the matter has to go back to the compositor's table, the chase has to be unlocked, alteration added or removed.

Some publishers make it amply clear in the contract that if the author's alterations exceed a certain limit the author will be liable to pay the additional cost of composing which the printer is going to charge if the alterations are too many. Most publishers though do not impose contractual clause of author's alterations, yet they do believe that an author who wants to rewrite his/her book after he/she has seen it in type should pay for this privilege.

No author, infact no body, likes to pay for ones mistakes or after thoughts. To minimise irritation, some publishers caution the author as soon as he starts departing from the manuscript when correcting proofs and make him aware that he is liable to be charged for excessive changes. If it is not too late, it is better to withdraw further matter from the press till it is revised afresh by the author.

It is important for authors to keep in mind that each letter, space and punctuation mark is represented by a little piece of metal (in hand and hot metal composing) which can neither be expanded nor contracted. On a larger scale the addition or alteration of several lines gives quite undue trouble and involves the transfer of type from one page to another. If new paragraphs are added they disturb many lines.

In order to avoid such a situation authors should be informed well in advance as to how to make changes in the text so that they cause least inconvenience and cost.

Authors should try to delete as much matter as they include so that the whole setting of matter is not disturbed. Authors should remember that original composing is charged by amount of type composed irrespective of the time involved but author's alterations are charged by the time the printers take to carry them.

The problem of author's alterations becomes more acute if the matter has been set by mono type or linotype. In such a case even if a word is to be added the whole line has to be recomposed.

To avoid such a situation, most publishers now provide their own house style directive to the authors so that manuscripts are prepared accordingly and there are fewer chances of changes in style. However, it is essential to settle these details before the printing is started rather than after whole work is set in type.

## HOW TO MARK PROOFS

Whether the matter is composed by hand or by hot metal machines; whether it is photocopy sheet from a film type setter; whether one is looking at the first proofs in the shape of a galleys or final proofs in the shape of imposed pages, proof reading is done and corrections are marked in the same consistent manner to find out if the compositor has followed the copy faithfully.

Proofs are read differently from reading a manuscript and should always be marked in a manner different from marking a typescript/manuscript. A typescript is usually marked in ink making corrections in between the lines (inter linear space). Proof corrections, on the contrary, are marked in the margins with an appropriate corresponding indication in the text by putting a caret (λ) mark. When a wrongly composed letter is altered or rewritten, a stroke is drawn through the incorrect portion and corrected version is written in the margin. Standard symbols to mark corrections are adopted for convenience and brevity so that they are uniformly understood without loss of time.

Speed reading technique would not help. One needs to read letter by letter. No matter how cautiously compositor has composed the matter, errors do escape detection by the compositor or keyboard operator. Good book production standards demand that any such mistake or omission and commission must be reduced to the lowest minimum though the ideal situation would be a publication with zero error.

Along the text matter page layout should also be checked. Mistakes do occur in running heads, tables, numbers, folios etc. All elements on a page should be properly and consistently checked. Reread the line where a mistake occurs once for the error and again for the problem of spacing.

Look at the proofs from designer's point of view. See that the text matter is not only correctly composed but also correctly adjusted. One should see alignment of lines, uniform spacing between the lines, consistency in type size and style.

Proofs should be read against dead copy—The copy from which the matter has been composed and set in type, to avoid any missing words or phrases. Dead copy is the only authoritative document to say what author wanted in print and in what form. Usage of spellings, proper names and other elements where inconsistency is possible can only be verified with the dead copy.

In some publishing houses it is the practice to send the manuscript from which the matter has been composed, to the author alongwith the first proofs. This is done to facilitate reading of proofs against the dead copy. The copy is kept for record so that in case of any confusion in proof reading this may be consulted for reference. The faithful reproduction of author's text can only be done with the dead copy. It is the only authority for checking spellings of proper names which are otherwise variously spelt.

## PROOF READER'S CHECKLIST

The following points are worth remembering while marking proof corrections.

1. All additions or changes in the text must be indicated by a caret (λ) mark.
2. All deletions in the text should be done by using a oblique(/) stroke.
3. All corrections should be reflected in the margin by recognised standard proof correction symbols as far as possible.
4. If only one letter or word is wrong, delete the letter or word and write the correct one in the margin.
5. If there are more than one corrections in one line, each correction should be followed by a stroke. For example x/e/t/
6. Always write horizontally in level with the line on which the error occurs.
7. A large correction should be rewritten legibly or retyped and attached or gummed with the proofs.
8. Cross out the passage that has been taken out or replaced.
9. Any addition should be made keeping in mind the length of the line.
10. Use pencil and not ink while correcting proofs.
11. If two persons are reading the same proof, use different coloured pencils.
12. Write corrections in clearly legible handwriting.
13. Corrections should be marked in a sequence from left to right.
14. Preferably, mistakes appearing on the left half of the composed page should be marked on left side margin and those appearing on the right half of the page should be indicated in the right hand margin.
15. All queries and instructions should be ringed.
16. Punctuation marks may be encircled to be noticed.
17. Differentiate comma (,) from apostrophe (') by using Appropriate symbol.
18. Distinguish superior figure and inferior figure.
19. Do not change inconsistent spellings in quoted material.
20. Check wrong font, wrong spacing, alignment, broken letter. These may not be printing errors but are irritants to good reading.

## PROOF READING MARKS

| *Correction Mark* | *Meaning* |
|---|---|
| ℘ | Delete |
| ⁐ | Close up |
| (℘) | Delete and close up |
| × | Replace broken letter or check |
| eq # | Equal space between words |
| # | Insert space |
| hr # | Insert hair space |
| ¶ | Begin new paragraph |
| no ¶ | Run paragraphs together |
| lc | Lower case |
| cap | Change to capital letter |
| sc | Set in small capitals |
| ital | Set in italic type |
| rom | Set in roman type |
| bf | Set in bold face |
| wf | Wrong font or set in correct type |
| ⊚ | Invert type |
| ⊐ | Move to right |
| ⊏ | Move to left |
| □ | Indent one em |
| ^ | Insert |
| ↩ | Run on or combine the paragraph |
| ⊓ | Raise up |
| ⊔ | Lover down |
| ] [ | Place in centre |
| = | Straighten type |
| ‖ | Align vertically |
| trs | Transpose |
| (sp) | Spell out |
| (stet) | Let it stand |
| ⊙ | Insert period |
| ^, | Insert comma |
| ∨' | Apostrophe or single quotation mark |
| ∨" | Double quotation mark |

| | |
|---|---|
| (;) | Semi colon |
| (:) | Insert colon |
| ⊢⊣ | Insert hyphen |
| $\frac{1}{n}$ | Insert en dash |
| $\frac{1}{m}$ | Insert em dash |
| ∨ | Superior figure |
| ∧₂ | Inferior figure |
| ⊏ | Take matter to beginning of next line |
| ⊐ | Take to the end of preceding line |

## QUALITIES OF A GOOD PROOF READER

A person who does the work of detecting errors and omissions in a typeset matter and marks the same with the help of proof correction symbols is called a proof reader. People who are not conversant with the process of book production cannot realise that good proof reading is not every one's cup of tea. To be a good and accurate proof reader one has to have certain inherent qualities of head and heart. Among many requirements that are necessary to make a person a good proof reader, the following figure prominently.

### *Thoroughly knowledgeable*

Knowledge of proof correction symbols is not enough. One should have knowledge of basics of typography, book design, and sufficient knowledge of various fields of arts and literature.

### *Linguistic competence*

The person should have proven proficiency in the language in which one operates. One should be fully conversant with the rules of grammar. A proof reader who is aware of his linguistic limitation is bad enough. But the one who is not is like the proverbial bull in a China shop spreading ruins wherever he goes.

### *Retentive memory*

A proof reader should not only have a sharp and searching eye, an alert mind and keen observation but also possess a retentive memory.

Inconsistency in spellings, word break ups, rendering of hyphenated words, abbreviations etc. can only be detected and corrected if the person has sharp retentive memory. One should be in a position to recollect on the subsequent occurrence of a word or phrase as to how it was rendered on previous occurrence.

*Familiarity with typography*

Knowledge of various type sizes, styles will enable a proof reader to recognise or detect composing hazards, broken type, wrong font, invert type etc. Knowledge of typography though not mandatory, certainly adds to the skills of a proofreader in returning error free proofs to the printer.

A heading may be rightly spelt but composed in a different type style or size inconsistent with other headings. Italics used may be of a different type size or small capitals may belong to different type family or style. Those and many more such irregularities can only be brought to the notice of the printer if proof reader has sound knowledge of typography.

## COPYHOLDER

Initial set of proofs is usually read by a team of two persons. One reading the copy and the other holding the proofs and marking corrections. The person who holds and reads the copy aloud to the person holding and marking the proofs is called the copy holder. Copy holder usually reads the dead copy. Copy holding therefore, is a function.

The involvement of two persons in the initial process of proof reading is the best way to detect mistakes and slightest variation in the composed matter from the copy. The method of involving a copy holder in the process of proof reading, helps the proof reader to concentrate on the proof copy without turning away from it to consult the copy (dead copy) from where the matter has been set in type.

Supposing the ideal situation exists, the copy holder is expected to perform as follows:

1. Strictly following the copy (dead copy).

2. Should have good pronunciation and ability to read fluently with uniform speed.
3. Should provide necessary pauses indicating punctuation marks. (Infact punctuation marks should also be read out).
4. Spellout difficult sounding and similar sounding words to differentiate them. For example, Ascent/Accent or Access/Assess.
5. Should be able to read all types of copies including handwritten copies with sufficient ease.
6. Should be conversant with proof reading symbols.

Ideally, proofs should be read this way. The prohibitive cost of employing two persons for this job is making the practice of using copy holder dearer and rarer.

It is not enough to only mark the mistakes, it is also essential for good proof reading to follow up the corrections and to see in the subsequent proofs that all the earlier corrections have been carried out.

# 17
# Paper

The word paper is derived from the Greek word 'Papyrus', an early Egyptian writing material extracted from papyrus plant.

## PAPER DEFINED

Paper is a material derived from wood, cloth, grass, or any other cellulose material which can be separated into its constituent fibres turned into pulp and manufactured into sheets [for such end purposes as printing, writing and wrapping].

It can also be defined as 'A web composed of vegetable fibres, roughly oriented and matted together so as to form a sheet'.

Though the technology of paper making may not be within the scope of this book, yet a brief outline of the story of paper and its process may help the reader to appreciate the craft and help in distinguishing varieties of paper and their qualities.

## BRIEF HISTORY

Paper making is an ancient craft. The writing on clay tablets and wooden strips was very slow and cumbersome process. Fabric, particularly silk was used as medium for writing. It is generally believed that Ts'ai.Lun a Chinese, invented paper around 105 A.D. The raw material used for paper making was old rags, hempwaste and bark of trees.

The invention of making ink from lamp black brought paper into further prominence and universal use. The art of paper making travelled from China to Japan and later to middle east and Europe.

The invention of movable type by Gutenberg of Mainz brought a revolution in the art of printing. The renaissance era in Europe created great demand for paper and paper mills were established in Europe.

The craft of paper making is said to have come to India through middle east but there are certain evidences which show that even before 15th century paper was in use in India. Palm leaf was commonly in use for writing. During the early days of British settlement paper was imported from England. In the beginning of 18th century a paper mill was established in India.

## RAW MATERIALS

The process of paper making can be explained as the addition of water to wood pulp, which is then passed through machines which progressively extract water and dry the moving 'web' of paper, at the same time causing separate fibres in the pulp to unite, giving strength to the paper.

The explanation given in the above paragraph may lead us to believe that wood is the only raw material needed for making paper. This is only half true. A variety of raw materials is available and used for making paper of different strength, smoothness and surface. Raw materials, commonly used for making paper can be enumerated as follows:

1. *Vegetable Cellulose:* The basic raw material of paper is carbohydrate cellulose produced by vegetables. Natural cellulose fibres which are available in many vegetables and plants are extracted by mechanical or chemical means. The amount of chemical action in extracting the cellulose from other organic substances decreases the durability of paper. Of the possible sources of cellulose fibres, more important are, wood, cotton, bamboo, grass, straw. The quality of paper depends upon the quality of the fibres used in the process of paper making.

2. *Rags or Cotton:* Cotton fibre is the longest and with minimum of impurities. But as rags it accumulates large number of impurities. Even as rags it is capable of becoming the raw material for superior quality of paper because of quality of cellulose.

3. *Esparto grass:* Esparto grass is also used as a basic component together with wood pulp for making very superior quality of paper. Esparto paper with special coating and finish is ideal for picture magazines. The surface of esparto paper depends upon the finish, sizing or calendering.

4. *Wood:* Natural wood is another basic ingredient of paper making. Wood paper is made from soft as well as hard wood. Soft wood papers are stronger as against papers made from hard wood as soft wood contains longer fibres and hard wood yields short fibres.

Normally wood papers are brittle and can be easily torn. Though wood is a natural product, but due to its indiscriminate use for paper making and other works of civil development, this natural resource is fast depleting and becoming scarce.

5. *Paper Waste or Broke:* Fast depleting natural raw materials have compelled us to look for alternatives to serve as substituted input for paper making. The process of recycling paper waste into paper has come as an alternative to natural fibres.

The paper waste, scrap of books and newspapers also known as 'Broke' can be used as raw material for making recycled paper. Because of many impurities which need to be removed from the scrap, the paper thus made is of inferior quality and weaker in strength and durability.

## PROCESS OF PAPERMAKING

The process of paper making involves the following operations:

1. Pulping
2. Beating
3. Loading
4. Sizing
5. Colouring

1. *Pulping:* Pulping or conversion of basic raw materials into pulp is the first operation in the process of papermaking. Pulping means transformation of raw materials such as rags, grass, wood into a slushy mass. It involves cutting of raw materials into small bits, boiling it and beating it to form a pulp.

The wood pulp can be made mechanically and chemically.

(i) *Mechanical method:* Under this process the logs are cut into small uniform size. These chips are forced against a revolving grind stone in hot water. The process separates the fibres in the wood. In mechanical method certain impurities remain in the pulp and therefore, cannot be used for making strong paper.

(ii) *Chemical method:* In preparation of pulp by using chemicals as against mechanical force, the length of the fibres can be maintained and stronger paper can be made out of the pulp. In this process, the wood is cut into small chips and boiled in a chemical solution. The process dissolves the impurities and leaves behind the fibrous pulp. The wood pulp is then screened and washed. The chemicals used are caustic soda or bisulphate of lime. After the wood has been reduced to pulp it passes through various processes to clean and purify it. The chemicals remaining in the pulp are thoroughly washed. The lumps formed during pulping are broken by rotating drums. This is done to get a smooth consistent thoroughly dissolved pulp. The broken material is then bleached. The bleaching agents (chemicals) are drained out.

2. *Beating:* The resultant stock (processed fibre) is then beaten in a beater. By beating fibres are torn apart and reduced to very tiny fragments. Beating is a process in which stock is passed through a stationary and rotary blades. The amount of beating determines the quality of paper. But before pulp is transformed into paper, loading, sizing and colouring is added to the beaten stock.

3. *Loading:* Minerals and other fillers added to the furnish of a paper is known as loading. It is done to make paper fit for writing. The gaps between the fibres are filled with some minerals to give it a smooth surface.

4. *Sizing:* The process of sizing is very essential for preparation of writing paper. Sizing is done to reduce the porosity of paper by applying glazing or coating material such as starch, glue, clay etc. The process of applying glazing material is called *sizing.* Sizing improves the hardness of the paper.

5. *Colouring:* In order to give a certain tinge of colour to the final product, sometimes, dyes and colours are added to the pulp during the beating operation so that a uniform colour is achieved.

## THE PROCESS

After the wood or rags or grass has been reduced to pulp and has passed through the various processes mentioned above and cleaned, bleached, loaded and sized, it is ready to be made into paper.

The pulp or stock is then fed on to the vibrating mesh or wire of paper machine. The excess water in the stock or pulp is drained away. The remaining water is removed by suction process.

Because of movement of mesh fibres tend to lie in the direction of flow and grains of the paper are thus formed. The cylinder wire roll provided in between the suction boxes to remove the remaining water, is called *Dandy roll.*

Dandy roll is also used in the process of papermaking to impress finished design, water marks or another marks upon the paper. The dandy roll determines the kind of weave or design that will appear on the finished paper and such matters whether or not the paper will bear water mark or trade mark.

The largely dried stock is then passed over to a felt blanket on to a series of rollers which by heat and pressure squeeze out a large part of water. The remaining moisture is removed by hot drums.

The paper then is ready for calendaring—a process by which paper is passed through rolls of calender to get smoothness, polish and required thickness and strength. Calendering is also a moisture removing device. After passing through calender rolls paper is wound on reels which may later be converted into sheets.

## KINDS OF PAPER

Paper is available in large varieties of finishes, qualities and weights, which can be put to variety of uses. Sometimes the same kind of paper may be used in variety of ways. The efficiency of production manager lies in his ability to match the quality of paper with the process of printing. The description of kinds of paper in the following paragraphs may give an idea about their distinct characteristics.

The most commonly used varieties of paper are:

1. *Antique:* It is a kind of printing paper with rough and textured finish. It is pulpy and fluffy. The texture of this paper is loose. It resembles handmade paper in appearance. Because of its bulk, a book with lesser number of pages may look voluminous. Because of its uncalendered surface it is not suitable for half tone blocks or fine line blocks. Since it absorbs ink quickly it is more suitable for letterpress. It comes in variety of finishes.

2. *Art Paper:* It is a smooth-finish paper which is acquired by coating of China clay and other adhesives. Coating is done on one or both the sides. Coating remains on the surface of the paper. When

printing is done, ink does not penetrate into the fibrous part of the paper and therefore gives fine results for printing of half tone illustrations. The paper, because of its attractive finish, is generally used for printing publicity literature. These days mat finish art paper is also made. Heavily loaded clay makes it less durable. It cracks easily when folded and sticks in damp conditions.

3. *Bond Paper:* Bond paper (also called bank paper) is a rough, strong and durable paper mainly used for typing or for writing with other instruments mainly for office use. Its durability is due to large percentage of rag contents. A costly paper usually *water marked*-having a trade name or logo impressed into the surface of paper by a dandy roll during the manufacturing process. A slightly lighter paper of this variety is called 'Bank Paper'.

4. *Book Paper:* The paper commonly used for pages of the book is classified as book paper. It is a paper of durable quality. Book paper is often surface sized to make it suitable for offset printing. The quality of book paper has deteriorated during the past few years because of its mass use and even less durable acidic papers are being used as book paper.

5. *Cartridge Paper:* It is a hard, tough class of paper made with a rough surface. Available in many grades, it is particularly useful for drawings. Offset cartridge though made for offset work can be used for letterpress printing also. Fine line blocks and half tone blocks can be printed with equal ease on cartridge paper.

6. *Cover Paper:* A slightly thicker and durable quality of paper available in wide varieties of finishes, textures and colours is called cover paper. It is used for cover material of books and other publications. Cover paper is available in special finishes like linen, leather finish, plain and matt and comes in variety of colours.

7. *Imitation Art Paper:* It is a cheaper quality of art paper heavily loaded with clay. Clay or filling medium is added at pulp stage before paper is made into sheets. The pulp is made dried and calendered the usual way but loading is done upto 30 percent of total weight of the paper. Because of larger clay contents it is also a weaker and less durable paper. As it has smoother surface it is also used for printing of half tone illustrations.

8. *India Paper or Bible Paper:* The special characteristics of this paper is that it is very thin and at the same time very strong and

opaque. Because of its compactness, it is used for printing Bibles, dictionaries and encyclopedias. A book printed on India paper will be at least three times lighter than a book of the same size printed on an ordinary book paper. It has acquired its name as India paper because of its Asian origin.

9. *Machine Finished Paper:* A paper on which the surface is sized and calendered while actually in the machine. Sometimes extra calendering is done to achieve smoother surface. This kind of paper is less porous and prevents fluid inks from spreading.

10. *Machine Glazed Paper:* This variety of paper is glazed on one side and rough on the other. Glossy finish in machine glazed paper is obtained by drying against the polished surface on heated cylinder of a paper machine.

11. *Map Litho Paper:* This variety of paper is used for printing by offset lithography. It has a smoother surface. This paper has its limitation that it can not print good halftone by letterpress. It is widely used for books, magazines etc.

12. *Newsprint:* This paper made from wood pulp is the cheapest kind of printing paper. It is brittle and less durable. It is used for printing of newspapers and other materials not of lasting value like handbills, pamphlets etc. It usually has rough surface (though glazed newsprint paper with smooth surface is also available) and can not give good results for line blocks and very coarse half tones.

13. *Offset Paper:* Infact any paper suitable for offset litho printing is called offset paper. It is well sized and slightly rough surfaced and less affected by moisture. This paper can print with good results line and half tone illustrations. This is used in letterpress also. This is also called plain paper.

14. *Super Calendered Paper:* This is a glossy finished paper of similar quality as machine finished paper. Extra finish is obtained by a calendering stack with alternate hard steel rollers and soft rollers which impart a high gloss finish to paper as it slips between them. This variety of paper is capable of providing good image reproduction.

There are unlimited varieties of paper available and may be used for purposes other than the ones mentioned above. But these are some of the varieties of paper commonly used in book publishing.

## PAPER SIZES

The ultimate unit of paper on which the book is printed is usually a sheet of paper. The sheet when folded once, twice, thrice or more times gives standard subdivisions and multiples of a broadside sheet. In order to understand standard book sizes it is necessary to know about standard sheet sizes out of which subdivisions are derived.

A standard quantity unit of paper is a ream. A ream consists of 500 sheets. In the field of book production paper is known by two names.

1. *Size of the Sheet:* The name given to a sheet size with a standard fixed length and width such as 'Royal', 'Demy', 'Crown' etc. For example 'Crown' means a sheet of paper 15in × 20in.

2. *Subdivision of Sheet size:* It is arrived at by multiplying the standard size or subdividing the standard size by folding it once or twice or more times to arrive at the required size. Double crown would mean double the standard size of crown ie. 20in × 30in. Alternately crown octavo would mean that crown sheet has been divided into eight by successively folding across the longer size to get page size of 5in × 7½in.

Each fold of the sheet is known by a particular name and gives a specific subdivision of a sheet size. The main subdivisions are:

1. *Broadside:* A sheet of paper of any size unfolded used for printing is called broadside or open sheet. A broadside sheet has two page (sides). It is generally used for printing maps and illustrations.

2. *Folio:* When a standard size sheet is folded once it gives two leaves or four pages it is called, Folio. The folding is done in the middle of the longer side of sheet. Folio is half the size of the broadside sheet.

3. *Quarto:* It is a page one quarter of the traditional broadside sheet size. When the sheet is folded twice it gives four leaves or eight pages. It is achieved by dividing shorter size of the sheet by two and the longer side of sheet also by two.

4. *Octavo:* It is a term used for a book made from sheets which have been folded three times, each sheet forming eight leaves or sixteen pages. The octavo size from a broadside sheet would be derived by the smaller side by two and longer side by four. For example octavo of double crown (20 in × 30 in) would be 10 in × 7½ in.

5. *Sixteen mo:* The term is used for a book size or a sheet subdivision which is arrived at by dividing each side of the sheet in four. It gives 16 leaves or 32 pages.

6. *Double:* A sheet which is double the size of the broadside sheet of any size is called a 'double', For example when demy size is 17½in × 22½ in. double demy would be 22½ in × 35in. This is arrived at by multiplying the shorter side of a broadside sheet.

7. *Quad:* In paper terminology quad is a name given to a sheet which double the size of the shorter and longer side of any broadside sheet. The Quad size is arrived at by multiplying shorter side of the sheet by two and longer side of sheet also by two. For example Quad demy would be 35in × 45in. Demy size of the sheet being 17½ × 22½ in.

8. *Section:* A folded sheet after deriving the required page size is called a section. In different paper sizes the number of pages in a section would vary. For example a section of Quarto size would be of eight pages whereas a section of octavo size would have 16 pages.

The following list gives the most commonly used papers, their multiples and subdivisions. All sizes are in inches.

| *Name* | *Broadside* | *Double* | *Quad* | *Quarter* | *Octavo* |
|---|---|---|---|---|---|
| Crown | 15 × 20 | 20 × 30 | 30 × 40 | 7½ × 10 | 5 × 7½ |
| Demy | 17½ × 22½ | 22½ × 35 | 35 × 45 | 8¾ × 11¼ | 5½ × 8¾ |
| Fool Scape | 13½ × 17 | 17 × 27 | 27 × 34 | 6¾ × 8½ | 4¼ × 6¾ |
| Imperial | 22 × 30 | 30 × 40 | 44 × 60 | 11 × 15 | 7½ × 11 |
| Medium | 18 × 23 | 23 × 36 | 36 × 46 | 9 × 11½ | 5¾ × 9 |
| Royal | 20 × 25 | 25 × 40 | 40 × 50 | 10 × 12½ | 6¼ × 10 |

Subdivisions and multiples of a broadside sheet

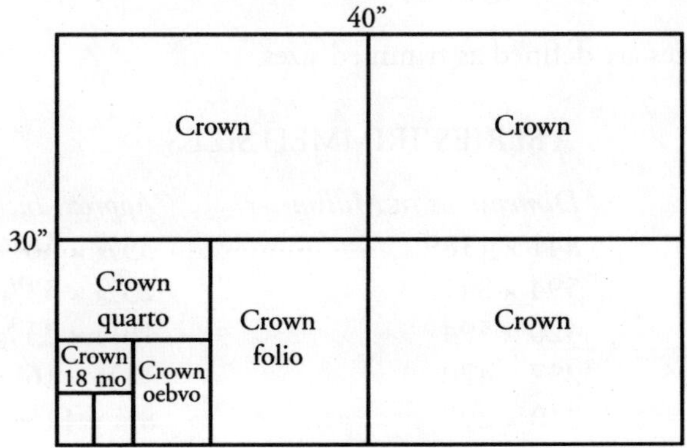


Quad Crown Sheet

## ISO PAPER SIZES ( METRIC PAPER SIZES)

Some of the varieties of paper had very small difference in size. In order to standardise the variations, International Standards Organisation (ISO) defined three series of paper sizes namely A, Band C Untrimmed size of A0 measures one square meter. A series paper is mainly used for printing books etc.

An important feature of metric subdivision is that sides of each sheet always stay at the rate of 1 : $\sqrt{2}$ . Therefore, a size below a particular number (Subdivision) will just be half of the upper number. The following figure will illustrate the point.

AO Size of Sheet-Area / Square Meter

A1
A2
A5
A6
A3
A4

Dimensions 841 mm × 1189 mm
Side Ratio 1 :$\sqrt{2}$

In A series sizes are defined as trimmed sizes.

### A SERIES TRIMMED SIZES

| *A Series* | *Dimensions in Millimeter* | *Approx. Inches* |
|---|---|---|
| A 0 | 841 × 1189 | 33⅛ × 46¾ |
| A 1 | 594 × 841 | 23⅜ × 33⅛ |
| A 2 | 420 × 594 | 16½ × 23⅜ |
| A 3 | 297 × 420 | 11¾ × 16½ |
| A 4 | 210 × 297 | 8¼ × 11¾ |
| A 5 | 148 × 210 | 5⅞ × 8¼ |

## PAPER CALCULATION, WEIGHT AND BULK

In order to avoid wastage in ordering paper and estimating costs, it is necessary to have an approximate accurate idea as to how much paper would be required for a given book if decision about the number of pages and size of the edition has been finalized. The following details need to be worked out to calculate paper quantities for a given edition.

1. Number of pages in the book (144, 272, 336 etc.)
2. Size of sheet (Demy, Crown, Royal etc.)
3. Size of the book (page) (Quarto, octavo etc.)
4. Size of the edition (1000 copies, 2000 copies etc.)
5. Percentage of spoilage (3% or 5% depends upon the number of colours and process of printing).

*Paper calculation:* Paper quantities are calculated in terms of reams of paper.

A ream is of 500 sheets. For calculation paper in reams the following method may be employed:

(Number of pages in the book × Number of copies to be printed) ÷ Number of pages in a section × 500 (Ream)

(Number of pages obtained by subdivision of a sheet size)

*Example*

How many sheets (in reams) in demy will be required for printing of 2000 copy edition of 368 pages book to be printed in octavo size (5½" × 8¾)

*Solution*

In this case we have the following information:

| | | |
|---|---|---|
| 1. | Number of pages in the book | 368 |
| 2. | Size of the sheet | Demy (17½" × 22½") |
| 3. | Book Size | Octavo |
| 4. | Section (Number of pages derived out of one sheet) | 16 |
| 5. | Number of Copies to be printed | 2000 |

Now let us apply the formula:

$$\frac{368 \text{ (Pages in the book)} \times 2000 \text{ (copies to be printed)}}{16 \times 500}$$

(Number or pages in a section) (Sheets in a ream)

So we get, $\frac{368 \times 2000}{16 \times 500}$ = 46000 Sheets or 92 Reams

The figure is without spoilage or wastage. To this figure a certain percentage of spoilage or wastage is added. Spoilage varies according to the number of colours, process of printing, make-ready and size of the edition.

Sometimes a publisher has to decide the size of the edition on the basis of the paper stock already available. In such a situation, if one knows the size of the sheet and page size alongwith the number of pages, one can calculate the number of copies that can be printed out of that available stock.

*Example*

How many copies of 128 pages book can be printed if the size of the page is demy octavo and 8000 sheets of demy are available in block.

*Solution*

In this example we know that

1. The Size of the sheet is demy *i.e* 17½" x *22½*"
2. The Size of the book pages in demy octavo *i.e.* 5½" x 8¾"
3. There are to be 16 pages in a section.
4. Number of pages in the book are 128

The solution, therefore, would be as follows:

$$\frac{\text{Number of pages per sheet} \times \text{Number of sheets available}}{\text{Pages in the book}}$$

Therefore the answer would be: $\frac{16 \times 8000}{128}$ = 1000 copies

## WEIGHT

Weight in printing parlance means the weight of paper in pounds or kilograms. It is important for the production manager to have knowledge about the weight of the paper being selected as most paper mills sell paper by weight.

In simple terms a 25 kg. paper means that 500 sheet of that paper (called a ream) in certain size (basic size) would weigh 25kg.

Paper weight is also known as substance. It is defined as the weight in grammes of one square meter of the paper. It is measured in grams per square meter or called GSM of paper.

The weight of the paper in a pile, therefore, would be equal to the product of the paper substance *i.e.* area of sheet and number of sheet in that pile.

To find out the weight of one ream of paper containing 500 sheets in a given size the following formula is applied

$$\text{Divided by } \frac{\text{GSM} \times \text{Size of the sheet in sq. meter} \times 500}{1000}$$

$$\text{To put more simply: } \frac{\text{GSM}}{2} \times \text{size of the sheet in sq. meter.}$$

*Example:* Find out the weight of one ream of 80 GSM paper in 38cm x 50cm size.

$$\textit{Solution: } \frac{80 \times 0.38 \times 0.50 \times 500}{1000} = 7.6 \text{ kg.}$$

In the above example we have calculated that the weight of 500 sheets of 80 GSM paper in 38cm × 50cm as 7.6 kg. In order to calculate the weight of paper in different size with the same G.S.M. The following formula may also be applied.

$$\div \frac{\text{Known weight of paper} \times \text{Required Size}}{\text{Size of the sheet (area) on the basis of which previous weight has been arrive}}$$

Now if the 80 GSM paper in 38cm x 50 em weight 7.6 kg. The weight of paper in 50 cm x 62.5 cm would be calculated *as* follows.

$$\text{Divided by: } \frac{\underset{\text{(Known weight)}}{7.6\text{ kg}} \times \underset{\text{(Required size of sheet)}}{50\text{ cm} \times 62.5\text{ cm}}}{\underset{\text{(Area of sheet whose weight has already been calculated)}}{38\text{ cm} \times 50\text{ cm}}}$$

$$\text{Therefore: } \frac{7.6 \times 50 \times 62.5}{38 \times 50}$$

$$\text{or } \frac{7.6 \times 50 \times 62.5}{38 \times 50} = \frac{23750}{1900} = 12.5 \text{ kg.}$$

## BULK OR CALIPER

Paper thickness is described in terms of number of pages may be to an inch or pages per inch. The term is also used to indicate the thickness of a book. Bulk is also known as *Caliper.* It is measured in thousandths of an inch.

It is desirable to know the thickness of the book in advance so that the actual size of the cover/jacket and area of spine (back of the book) may be finalized. The jacket design will loose its impact if the bulk of the book is not measured in advance.

Bulk or caliper is an important factor in deciding the book format. A short manuscript may be given a bulky look or a bulky manuscript may be given a manageable look by using a thicker or thinner paper respectively. Calendered sheet will have less bulk than others of the same weight.

## SELECTION OF PAPER

A bewildering variety of paper is available to a publisher for book work. As we have seen in this chapter that from unglazed newsprint to coated art paper can be used for book work. The decision to select one particular kind for a given book will be the result of various considerations. Paper being the main constituent in the cost of production of a book, the production manager can show his expertise in selecting paper which is economical but at the same time can give desirable results.

The selection of paper, therefore, is guided by the following factors.

1. *Size of the sheet and size of the book*

As we knew that standard size of a book is derived from a standard size of sheet by folding it once, twice or more times. If we choose unconventional size for a book, we may have to waste a large amount of paper if the sheets are not available in its multiple from where subdivision of book size can be derived. Therefore, the size of the book will determine the size of sheet in a given quality of paper.

2. *Durability*

As we have seen in chapter on raw materials the durability of paper depends upon the raw material from which it has been made. Paper made from rags is more durable than paper made from woodpulp. Similarly there are acid free papers which are more longer lasting than acidic varieties of paper. Durability also means higher folding endurance. Certain varieties of paper such as news print lack strength and tear easily when folded frequently.

3. *Grain Direction*

The direction in which most of the fibres in a sheet of paper run is called grain direction. Fibres running parallel with the larger side of sheet is known as long grain and when the fibers run along the shorter side it is called short grain. Where paper is folded against the grain direction, it tends to crack or folds raggedly. But when folded in the grain direction, fibres tend to fold evenly and smoothly. A book which is bound against the grain resist opening. The problem of paper stretch is minimised with a long direction sheet. It also helps registering of multi coloured job.

4. *Process of Printing*

Suitability of paper to the process of printing is another essential consideration. For example, any plain paper may be suitable for letter press printing. But for lithography, paper with hard surface is preferred. In gravure process fine screen can be printed on any kind of paper. Shade of the paper will, however, vary the reproduction. In most cases the shade of paper used is white but if the illustrations are bright than off white paper may be preferred. Paper made from woodpulp is cheapest and brittle and therefore used for newspapers. Coated art paper is costlier and gives finer reproduction of illustrations and is, therefore, used for printing of halftone illustrations.

5. *Thickness* or *Bulk*

In the preceding pages we have noticed that there are certain varieties of paper which have more thickness than other varieties of paper. If the volume of the manuscript is small and publisher wants to give it a bulkier look one may opt for *antique* paper which is 30% to 40% thicker than ordinary printing paper. Alternately, if the manuscript is voluminous and it is of lasting value, the choice may fall on *Indian paper* which is very thin and still very strong.

6. *Weight* or *Substance of paper*

As paper is sold by weight, therefore, a lighter paper will cost much less than a heavier paper. But the weight of paper should be relevant to the nature of the book. For example, a text book for college students may be printed on a paper with lighter substance or GSM but a children book would need a heavier paper with more weight.

7. *Shade of Paper*

The shade of paper, when available in more than one variety may also be considered. Paper is available in bright, white, off white and creamy shade. The option for a particular shade may be exercised keeping in mind the nature of the book. Certain papers change shade with the passage of time.

8. *Suitability* to *printing link*

Printing ink is made of colouring matter and a medium to hold pigments of colour. Inks dry by absorption into paper or by evaporation. On a porous surface the absorption will be faster as against a smoother surface. Absorption factor, therefore, is very important. On a non-porous paper inks dry either by evaporation or by chemical change. Both these processes are slow. High speed printing may, therefore, pose problem of *smudging.* The absorption and porosity depend on the kind of fibres used and treatment given during the process of paper making.

9. *Opacity of Paper*

The quality of opaqueness in a paper is another factor which plays a vital role in the selection. Opacity is measured in % with around 90% being an average printing paper. Opacity is also related with the bulk of a paper. Coated papers have more opacity than uncoated paper. Papers coated on both sides are very opaque because of two layers of clay. The problem of 'show through' becomes apparent in a less opaque paper. Because of lower percentage of opacity printed image on one side is visible from the other side and this hinders the readability of the book.

Similar considerations must also be kept in mind while ordering or selecting paper for jacket and other materials.

# 18

# Book Binding

Books are repositories of knowledge and wisdom. They are mirror of our culture and civilisation. They are record of our history and have been treasured and preserved from time immemorial. Not only that, books are the most important tool of teaching and learning.

## NEED

There is, therefore, a need for preserving them for as longer period as possible. Binding provides the first step in preserving them in the shape and form in which they are created. The main purpose of binding, therefore, is to hold pages of a book and protect them.

Multiplicity of books published in the post Gutenberg period made it necessary to identify one book from the other. So binding started serving another purpose also—of identification of the contents by putting the name of the author and title of the book on the binding itself. When books became a commercial commodity it necessitated to make their binding attractive and inviting.

## BINDING DEFINED

Book binding can be defined as a method of folding and uniting leaves of paper within protective covers. It is a process of fastening together printed or plain sheets of paper and enclosing them within a protective cover in such a way as to facilitate reading and viewing.

The process of book binding can also be defined as an art or technique of securing printed or plain sheets of paper in a loose or folded form in a proper sequence in order to protect them from dirt and damage during handling and storing.

Binding is a link in the production process. If binding is not done adequately and securely, in the required style and strength, whole labour on designing and publishing a book may go waste as the product will not last long.

## BRIEF HISTORY OF BINDING

The craft of book binding precedes the invention of printing by movable type. Manuscripts written on palm leaves were given a special treatment so that they could be preserved for a longer period. This was perhaps the first attempt by man towards preserving the written material for posterity. From this urge, grew the techniques for holding the written material together which in later days came to be known as binding.

The invention of papyrus by Egyptians in 4000 B.C. is an important landmark in the growth and development of binding technique. Since papyrus was created with great skill from the papyrus plant a greater need to preserve the labour was felt. Books were produced in scrolls. At each end of the scroll a roller was attached. The two rollers served as the binding mechanism for holding and reading the scrolls.

In scrolls, lines were written upto the full length of the scroll thus making it mandatory on the reader to roll at one end and unroll at the other while one is reading through the line and again reverse the process to read the second line. Even where the lines began to be written in columns instead of the length of the scroll, reading still was a cumbersome process.

To ease this problem, the pages were folded instead of wound on a roller. This type of arrangement of written material was known as *Concertina* and with this, folding came into being. To make the use of this folded concertina more convenient the back folds of the books thus folded began to be fastened and that became the stitching which is an important process in modem day binding.

The use of parchment—an early writing and book binding materi.al made from skin of sheep, goats and other animals—made it possible to create book with flat folded sheets. Because of its strength and finish it made it possible to write on both the sides of the leaves and written leaves were folded, forming a section and many such sections were stitched together and thus became a section which is an important aspect of today's binding. The sheets were tied together with a lace, passing through the hole made on the back of the sheets and kept between two boards. The place of rollers in scrolls was taken over by the boards. Thus, covers with a lace became the oldest form of stitching.

During the year 105, Ts'ai Lun, a Chinese invented the paper. The raw materials used were said to be old rags, hemp waste, bark of trees etc. In short span of time the craft of paper making spread throughout China and neighbouring areas.

The invention of writing ink in 400 AD was another landmark which revolutionised the writing of books. The ink was made of lamp black, burnt ivory, charcoal etc.

The invention of paper coupled with the invention of writing ink gave an impetus to the writing and preserving of books. Since the writing was done by hand and scribes who used to write books, took a long time to complete one book, only very rich and affluent people could afford to keep books. Rich owners, therefore, lavishly spent money in protecting and preserving the books.

This was the era of decorated covers. Goldsmiths and silver smiths were involved in decorating the covers which were made either of wood or leather. Even inlay work where pieces of metal, gold and silver set with jewels were used to engrave blocks to make the cover beautiful. During this period binding was done by two types of people—one binder and the other decorator. Books were fewer and therefore, each book was bound separately. Sometimes each copy had individual design on the covers.

*Invention of Printing*

Then came the invention of printing by movable type and followed by the renaissance period when the need for books multiplied and invention of printing made it easier to print several copies of one book at much less time. Speed, therefore, became the hallmark of binding and the glorious period of individualistic decorative covers took a backseat.

*Islamic Influence,*

In the West book binding of *Codices—books* using wooden blocks as their protecting covers—had reached a standard of opulence and excellence in the ancient and middle ages. The craft of binding during this period had reached the level of perfect art. In the twelfth century bindings with elaborate and decorative leather covering and tooled with pictorial and geometrical designs were produced in Paris.

The book binding art reached its zenith during the 15th century and after. Due to invention of printing, there was tremendous demand for printed literature and the art and craft of book binding flourished in these centuries. During this period the cover material was generally made of wood and covering was done with leather, silk, velvet and tooling was done with gold and silver. The binding in these days was so attractive that people started possessing books because of its rich binding rather than the contents. Many examples of such bindings exist even today.

Some researchers believe that gold tooling and decorative motifs is the gift of islamic influence, though there are some examples of gold tooling binding covers during the 12th century.

In the process of gold tooling, the surface of the leather was first painted with treated egg white or 'glair' as it was called, over which the gold leaf was placed. The tool with decorative motifs was heated and impressed into the leather covering through the gold leaf. The heat cooked and set the egg white bonding the leather with the pattern. Gold and silver having become too precious these days tooling is done with paper coated with golden and silvery pigments.

### *Renaissance and After*

The invention of printing by movable type by Johann Gutenberg in 1438 revolutionised the printing industry. Development of paper manufacturing machines increased the output of books to a very high level. Wooden boards, gold and silver tooling and other embellishments began to give way to binding methods which were cheaper and faster so that books could reach larger number of people in shorter time. Until now printer was his own binder but as the speed and number of books produced increased, book binding became a separate trade.

In the years that followed, printing industry developed many fold. High speed machines for composing and printing were invented and put to use. This necessitated the need for high speed binding to cope with the printing speed. Thus were invented different kinds of machines which helped high speed binding of books to meet the challenge of the time.

*Development of Machines*

Some of the machines that were developed during the 19th and 20th century include invention of paper cutting machine (1840) by one Wilson. The machine was known as Guillotine machine, which could cut a pile of paper sheets in one stroke. Folding machine was invented in the year 1850. Improvements to this machine were made in the following decades.

In the year 1850 Starr invented the rounding and backing machine. Machines for gathering and collating the gathered sections were also invented and put to use. In the last decade of 19th century casing machine was also invented.

*Binding in India*

The art of binding in India is as old as books. During the days when scriptures were written on *Bhojpatras* and arranged in loose leaf form, a covering of hard and thick material was provided which served as the outer protective covering of the scripture. The examples of scrolls and other forms of ancient books with covering material are also available.

The art of binding in the conventional style with tooling had arrived in India with Persian influence during the 13th century. During the Mughal period the art of leather binding with medallians and corners stamped with calligraphic and geometrical designs with gold tooling reached its zenith. Simultaneously the use of painted and illustrated wooden covers far ancient Hindu, Jain and Buddhist manuscripts called *Pattas* also flourished.

Multifunctional binding machines are in operation these days. There are binding machines which contain complete assemblies required for various operations of binding. Machines have also been developed for perfect binding—a process in which signatures are trimmed into loose sheets, which are then glued.

Developments are still on to further improve the technology and achieve refinement in this craft which provides aesthetics to the art of book production.

## KINDS OF BINDING

A number of binding options are available these days. Decision to choose a particular type of binding will depend upon several factors. The most important among these is the economic factor. What cost a publisher can afford towards binding an edition of a title? Other factors include the subject, size, readership and expected span of life of the book. It is, therefore, necessary for a production man to know various options available and their suitability to the kind of publication to be bound.

Among the various varieties in which a book can be bound the following are most commonly used.

1. Saddle stitch
2. Side stitch
3. Lump or flexible binding
4. Perfect binding
5. Loose leaf or album binding
6. Mechanical binding
7. Case binding or edition binding
8. Reinforced library binding

1. *Saddle wire stitching*

This is an economical form of binding publications between 32 and 64 pages and sometimes more depending upon the size and bulk of the paper. Most of the magazines, journals and pamphlets are bound this way.

In this type of binding folded sections are placed one inside another. The pages will be imposed in such a way that first half of the top section contains the first pages and the last half of the section will contain the last pages. In other words the forme is locked up in such a manner that first pages are printed with the last pages. The machine on which binding is done looks like the saddle of a horse on which collated forms are put for stitching.

After the sections are gathered, the cover is placed on the top and stitching is done through the back and the triming is done from the rest of the thsee sides. Both power operated and hand operated machines are available. Saddle stitching is done either by wire staples or by continuous line of cotton stitches. The number of stitches will depend upon the size of the spine.

*Advantages and disadvantages*

Saddle wire stitching is very cost effective method of stitching small sized publications.

Pages in this type of binding open easily without arresting any folio margin in the binding.

Its limitations are:

It can not be used for bigger or bulkier publications.

If the size of publication is big stitches would not hold the pages for long. After some use pages will come off the stitches.

The wire may rust during humid conditions and damage the pages.

Since saddle wire stitched, publications do not have spine, their storage and retrieval in libraries becomes a problem.

Because of peculiar locking up of pages, the decision about this kind of binding can not be taken with regular imposing style.

2. *Side stitching*

In side stitching or side stapling, sections and formes are kept one after the other in one continuous sequence. Thus section of pp. 1-16 will be followed by section with pp. 17-32 and so on. Fewer operations are involved in this kind of binding. The gathered sections are put under the side stapling (stitching) machine. The number of staples will depend upon the length of the spine. The cover is either stapled alongwith the main publication or pasted on the spine after the sections have been stapled. Like saddle stitching, side stitching can also be done by thread instead of wire staples. The three sides are trimmed after the stapling has been completed.

*Advantages and disadvantages*

Side stitching is also a cheaper method of binding a publication.

It can be used for publications bigger in size than those used for saddle stitching.

Provision of pasting cover after the side stapling keeps the spine neat and wire staples do not show from out side.

The disadvantage of this binding is that cover usually comes off because it is held with the text pages only at stapled points and not all along the spine if not pasted over it.

A portion of folio margin is always arrested because of the staples and book does not lie flat on the table unless held by hands.

It is unsuitable for a publication which is required to be kept open for reference for longer periods.

3. *Limp binding or Flexible binding*

Limp binding is a, term used to denote a kind of binding in which binder's boards are made of flexible material and resulting covers limp or remain flexible rather than rigid. It is also known as flexible binding. It includes paper back bindings and limp covering material bindings of all types. The 'art card' or 'pulp board' which is lighter in weight than binder's board is used as cover material. Sometimes, plastic sheets are used as cover material to give an elegant and smooth finish to the binding.

Limp binding can be sewn or unsewn. Large number of school textbooks and other cheaper publications which require frequent handling are examples of sewn limp binding. Unsewn limp binding is used for publications which are known as mass market paper backs.

In limp binding, after the sheets are folded and gathered, sections are collated to check that gathered sections are in order. The book is sewn in sections with thread by hand or thread sewing machine. The cover is pasted on the spine. In limp binding, the spine of the book is kept flat. The sides are trimmed after attaching the cover.

*Advantages and disadvantages*

This is also a cost effective method of binding. Limp covers cut down the cost considerably.

Costlier hard cover books can be made available at cheaper price by using limp cover binding.

It also allows a book to lie flat on the table without holding it by hands.

Pulp card or art card being less strong and durable than the board, this binding does not last long.

In unsewn limp binding adhesive plays an important role. Strength of binding will also depend upon the text paper.

4. *Perfect binding or Adhesive binding*

Perfect binding is another name given to unsewn limp binding. In this process, after the sheets have been folded, gathered and collated, they are held tightly and a small portion of the spine is sliced off thereby turning the sections into individual pages. The trimmed spine is roughened or notched. One or two applications of adhesive are applied to the roughened spine and the adhesive layer is carried round a little way to the front and back of the book. This is done so that the cover when applied on the glued back, is held firmly.

The process of perfect binding involves application of some kind of flexible glue or quick drying adhesive. It is therefore also called adhesive binding.

Perfect binding, therefore, is a process in which signatures are trimmed into loose sheets, which are then glued together by applying some kind of fast drying adhesive to the spine of the book. The binding itself is glued directly to the spine of the book. The pages of the book are held together with the help of some glue or adhesive rather than sewn together. It is also known as *threadless binding.*

When binding is done by applying only one layer of adhesive to bind both the text pages and the cover it is called *one sheet* perfect binding. When glue is applied to the text spine to join text pages and again applied for the second time to attach the cover to the book it is called *two sheet* perfect binding.

Perfect binding has arisen from the need to keep the cost of books low. It was not possible to produce cheaper books with hard cover binding. This led to the advent of paper back editions of books during the 1940s. Once they were introduced in the market, they were instant success and now there are machines available where at one end sheets are fed and on the other end perfectly bound book is delivered.

Automatic and semi automatic machines are available which bind books at a very high speed. Fully automatic machines are fitted with gadgets with gathering and trimming facilities. In these machines folded sections are filled in the hopper feeder of gathering unit at one end of the machine and three knife trimmer at the other and deliver stacks of finished books.

In a semi automatic machine the gathered and collated books are fed into open clamps of the machine and processed further at a high speed. The books are delivered with creased cover duly attached. They are then trimmed at the head tail and fore edge either on a cutting machine (guillotine) or a three knife trimmer.

*Advantages*

The process of perfect binding is not only cheap but also very fast. This is used for a wide variety of paperback fiction and non fiction books where *price* and not durability is the main consideration. Other advantages of perfect binding include:

(i) Perfect binding book opens flat irrespective of the size.
(ii) The book can either be produced paper cover or cased in.
(iii) Binding is very flexible.
(iv) It can be produced in an uninterrupted work flow.

*Disadvantages*

Perfect binding also has some inherent disadvantages and constraints. Since there is no thread used in sewing the pages, these are held together with adhesive only. Therefore, the paper and the glue assume greater importance in the success or failure of the binding. Drawbacks of perfect binding are:

(i) The binding appears quite strong but before long glue perishes and pages fall apart.
(ii) Unless tropicalised adhesive is used, the binding comes off in hot climate.
(iii) Quality of adhesive has direct bearing on the strength of binding.
(iv) Every kind of paper is not suitable for perfect binding. Heavily coated art paper or super calendar paper is unsuitable to hold adhesive in this process. Therefore good quality smooth finished paper is not successful.
(v) Application of adhesive, accuracy of setting and absorvancy of paper are critical factors. Any variation in these may result in unstable binding.

5. *Loose leaf binding or Album binding*

In loose leaf binding, a publication consists of individual printed or illustrated sheets which are held together mechanically thereby allowing individual leaves to be replaced at convenience.

In this kind of binding printed sheets are punched and covered in a jacket or other covering material by means of a tape or ribbon. This arrangement facilitates the removal of out of date material and insertion of upto date matter. Publications like law reports, catalogues and some times membership directories are bound by these method.

For loose leaf binding there is no need to compose the material in the shape of a forme. The pages are, in any case, cut into individual leaves and punched at the back and tied together. Because of its appearance like an album, it is also known as album binding.

6. *Mechanical binding*

Mechanical binding has become very popular these days because of the ease and speed with which some publications can be bound. Various types of binding styles in this category are collectively known as mechanical binding.

In mechanical binding all individual pages of a publication are trimmed from all the four sides and a series of holes are punched near the spine at uniform intervals. A spiral spring shape wire is passed through these holes. This kind of binding allows the publication to open flat from any part of the book.

Another development in spiral wire binding is spico binding in which holding and fastening device is made of plastic. A small strip of uniform width emerging out of a thin plastic backbone is inserted into punched holes of the publication all along the spine. Unlike mechanical binding holes in spico binding are rectangular. Both wire spiral and plastic methods of binding are costlier as compared to other types like limp or flexible bindings.

*Advantages*

(i) Mechanical binding looks very neat and beautiful.

(ii) Pages and sheets can be arranged and rearranged at one's convenience.

(iii) The process is very fast as operations like stitching or gluing are not required.
(iv) It is very useful for binding of manuals, instruction books and workbooks.

*Disadvantages*

(i) As there are no sections in mechanical binding and individual sheets are held together with the help of spiral or plastic comb, pages have the tendency to get detached after frequent handling.
(ii) Any rough handling can damage the spiral as holes are punched at very dose to each other.
(ii) Because of the weight of spiral wire or plastic comb, the publication becomes unevenly balanced and not conducive to longer life.
(iv) Wire spiral or plastic comb, being fluffier than the main publication, causes difficulty in storage and retrieval of the publication from the stack of books.
(v) Books needing repeated references and frequent handling are not advised to be bound by this method.

7. *Case binding*

Case binding or edition binding is done in an assembly line process manually or with the help of machines. The process of case binding is divided into two parts. One—folding gathering, collating and sewing the sheets and two—preparing the case with covering material like card board and attaching the case.

In this process, the sections are sewn, cut backed, rounded, the spine is glued and lined up with first and second lining. A separate case is prepared with the help of board. The boards are cut according to the book size. The boards are covered using fabric or paper, rexin or leather. The inner side of the boards is covered by using paper covering in the shape of end papers which hold the cover on one side and the book block on the other. The sewn portion of the sections called book block is pasted into the case with the help of tapes or lining.

Quick mass binding of all copies of an edition where one copy of the edition is undistinguishable from the other is also called publisher's binding or edition/case binding. As the cover of binding is made of hard boards it is also called hard cover binding. The various operations of case binding are discussed in the following pages, step by step.

8. *Reinforced library binding*

When demand for mass book production had not arisen, binders put their skill in making strong durable bindings. Moreover books were owned by individuals and were not subject to frequent handling. Nowadays, the binding of books is done at much higher speed and at much lesser time. This leads to deterioration in the standards of binding and life of a bound book.

With the coming of library movement in the world and expansion of education, books exchange hundreds and thousands of hands and any weakness in book binding reduces the strength of binding requiring the book to be rebound. To meet this special challenge of frequent book use has given rise to another kind of binding known as Reinforced library binding. This is especially done for copies meant for library use. The purpose is to provide extra strength and durability to the book.

The term reinforce denotes to extra strength provided to the binding using Morocco (Goatskin with fine grain) instead of calf skin to cover the spine. Sewing is normally done on tapes and inserted in the splits of two boards used as casing.

The provision of French joint—a gap between the boards and spine where the leather is impaired is done by leaving a small space between the back edge of the board and the groove made by backing. It provides a greater area of covering material and facilitates the opening and closing of the book without putting any strain on the spine.

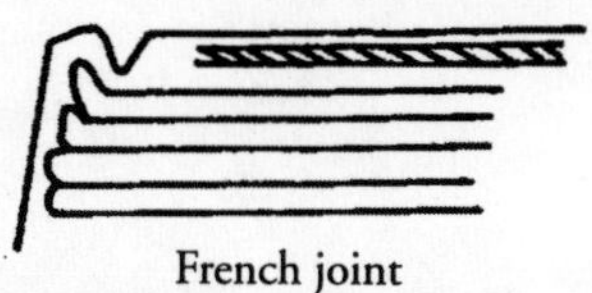

French joint

The size of the groove should be equal to the thickness of the boards used for case. A wider groove will weaken the binding and a narrower one hinders the free opening of the book. Reinforced library binding helps a bound book keep its shape and strength for a longer period.

## BINDING OPERATIONS

The ultimate unit on which a book is printed is a sheet of paper. These printed sheets form the basis of binding operations. After the binder has received the printed sheets for binding, these sheets having separate signatures are arranged and piled separately.

A signature is a single sheet of paper printed on both sides and which when folded and trimmed becomes a set of consecutive leaves and pages. When a sheet printed on both sides and folded once it gives two leaves and becomes a four page signature. Similarly where such a sheet is folded twice or three times it gives four leaves and eight leaves and becomes eight page and sixteen page signature respectively.

Before starting the binding operations one sheet from each pile is gathered folded and arranged in running continuous sequence and a dummy is prepared to assess the book bulk and to ascertain that all the signatures required for binding have been received. The dummy will also help in calculating the cover material needed as well as size of boards required for the case of the binding.

The sequence of operations in a hard cover (case binding) book is as follows:

*Book Block*
Folding
Bundling
Tipping
Gathering
Collating
Sewing
Nipping and pressing
Gluing
Trimming
Rounding and backing
Lining
Casing in- Attaching the boards
Pasting of endpapers

*Case making*
Preparation of cover material
Making a dummy-book bulk
board cutting
Pasting and making the case
Attaching the case

Some operations like folding, tipping, gathering collating etc. are common, irrespective of the kind of binding. Some later operations are eliminated and give place to other operations characteristic to a specific kind of binding. In hard cover binding the process is divided into two groups of consecutive operations. The operations like folding, gathering, collating and sewing are collectively called 'Sheet work', and the rest of the operations like gluing, trimming, rounding backing and attaching the case etc. are called 'forwarding'.

## FOLDING

Folding is an important aspect of binding. If folding is not done in order, the pages will not run consecutively. Folding depends upon the imposition or lockup style in which the pages have been printed. Folding can be done by hand or by buckle folding machine. Size of the publication is derived by folding a broadside sheet into required number of folds.

As already explained in the above paragraphs if a broadside sheet is folded once it will produce two leaves and four pages. The second fold would produce four sheets and eight pages (Quarto). Third fold would produce eight sheet (Octavo) and sixteen pages. Sometimes, if the paper used is of double the normal sheet size and also of very thin quality, another fold is given to acquire sixteen sheets (sixteen mo) and thirty two pages.

Care, therefore, needs to be taken while folding the printed sheets. Folding is generally done by the following methods:

1. *Folding* to *paper:* In this method sheets are folded exactly at the centre. The print may or may not register properly on the pages facing each other. This is also known as edge to edge folding as a sheet is folded exactly in half. Difficulty in registration is a common draw back with this kind of folding. This is usually done for cheap books. In this kind of folding margins may not remain uniform because of irregular registration.

2. *Folding* to *print:* This is done by laying one printed edge against the printed edge on the opposite side of page to ensure that pages are folded in exact registration. Exactness of margin is also taken into account. Unlike folding to pages (edge to edge) the edges of folded sheet may not fall exactly on each other. Any difference in margins is corrected at the time of trimming of the book. This method is also known as 'folio to folio' or typographical folding, The method is time

consuming if done by hand but gives quality results and is used for prestigeous and costly publications.

3. *Limp folding:* When more than one sheet is folded together or when four pages forme are collectively folded especially for covers and end papers, it is called limp folding.

## BUNDLING AND SMASHING

When sheets are folded certain air is trapped into the folded leaves making the folds fluffier than the front edges. The folded forms are therefore smashed in a press to flatten the folds. After all the sections are smashed all the formes are bundled separately and piled.

## TIPPING WRAPPING AND INSERTING

Tipping means insertion of additional printed sheets to already printed material or separately printed leaves pasted or tipped into a book. It is easier to paste pages on to the outside of a signature but pasting them in the middle like an illustration separately printed is a difficult and time consuming job. Tipping is done by applying glue and pasting edge to 1/8" inside running the length of the page.

Sometimes, a book is not printed in complete sections. A single leaf or a four page section is required to be pasted over the rest of the pages to complete a section. Such insertion is called *Wrapping.*

Enlarging a section by four or more pages by inserting them into a signature in the middle or elsewhere is called *Inserting.*

No matter extra pages are added to the main section by whichever description they are properly guarded so that they do not come off with slightest pull while handling. Guarding is a method of securing plates with the help of a guard which is usually a slip ¾ inch wide of paper sewn as any other section and plates are pasted on it.

## GATHERING

In this operation all the printed folded formes are kept on a long table in a reverse sequence. Last forme is kept in the beginning and first forme at the end of the table so that when these formes are gathered in that order, the gathered book appears in a correct sequence of pages. In hard binding the job of gathering is done with great care. Any mistake in gathering would result incomplete binding. Either one signature would be missing or there would be two signatures with same page numbers.

## COLLATING

The process of gathering the folded signatures and merging them in a sequence to determine the completeness of the book to be bound is called collating. This is done by placing a mark by the printer on the back of the fold of each signature to be gathered in a book. The marks are placed in such a sequence that a missing signature may be easily identified by the gap in the sequence of marks.

The importance of collating in the process of binding can not be under estimated. It is this operation which helps the binder to detect that there is nothing defective, duplicate or missing in a book as an incomplete book is of no value or use.

## SEWING

The essence of edition binding is sewing. This is done by thread, and other stitching materials like silk laces or nylon etc. The thread is carried through the back of the signature at three or four places depending upon the length of the section. Cotton, linen or lining cloth is used for tapes which are sewn alongwith the back of the spine of the book block. The thread, after passing through a section, is taken across to the next section by a 'kettle stitch'. The thread is carried up and down across the entire book.

This kind of stitch is done for cased-in binding. In cased-in binding, the case is prepared separately and the sewn and trimmed book is cased with it. In library binding when the book is taken away from sewing frame one or two inches of tape are left projecting from either side of the book and later pasted or inserted into the boards that forms the cover or case of the binding.

The two common ways of sewing are (1) hand sewing (2) machine sewing.

*Hand sewing:* This is done with the help of a sewing frame.

The frame consists of a bed with two uprights and cross bar which can be heightened or lowered by turning of a nut or screw. The sections of a book are placed in the frame. The sewing is done through saw cuts derived by ordinary carpenter's saw. These cuts should be sharp but not deep. If the cuts are deep and not neat the grip of the thread will remain weak and there is a possibility of glue filtering down when gluing and rounding off is done in the process of binding. Thickness of the thread should be in accordance with the saw cuts and thickness of section. The thread is passed through in saw cut in and out along the spine of the signature and taken out to pass through the second signature from the opposite side of the spine and the operation continues till the last signature has been sewn.

*Machine sewing:* To sew larger quantities, faster speed machines are used for sewing. Machine sewing also works on the principle of hand sewing except that the sewing is made up of a series of separate components each with its tape and two kettle stitches. Most common ways of machine sewing are:

*Saw in sewing:* In this, sewing is done by thin cord which fits into saw cuts, not leaving any projection in the back.

*Flexible Sewing:* In flexible sewing there are no shallow saw cuts. The thread passes through the cords duly encircling them. When set of two cords are used for such sewing and the thread passes through each cord, one by one, encircling each of the cord, it is called double flexible sewing. It is the strongest method of sewing the sections of a book.

*Tape sewing:* When tapes are used instead of cords it is called tape sewing.

## NIPPING AND PRESSING

When the sections are sewed they are given a heavy rapid squeeze to force out all air trapped into the folds of sewed sections. Because of trapped air folded edges swell and the back of the book block becomes thicker. Book block is placed between two metal plates called Jaws of the nipping machine to reduce the swelling caused by the stitching and to make the sewn sections easier to handle during subsequent operations. The process of ejecting air from the stitched sections to make the book block of uniform thickness is called nipping.

## GLUING

After the book has been sewn it is kept in between a pair of straw boards and held firmly in a laying press. The spine is knocked square. A coating of flexible glue is applied to the spine at this point so that the gap between the sections is also filled and the entire book block is held firmly.

Gluing operation needs to be done with care. If the glue is thick it may not run between the sections and if it is too thin it will pass through the saw cuts made for sewing the sections and spoil them. The book should be taken out of the laying press only after the glue is properly dried up. Any crimp or twist at the gluing stage will make it difficult to mend. The quality of glue should be such as may not crack or peel off while rounding and backing.

## TRIMMING

The book is now trimmed from the three sides. The machine used to cut the edges of the leaves is called 'Guillotine' or 'plough'. Generally one side at a time is cut. Three knife trimmer, cutting the three side, in one go is also available.

The work of trimming the book is done with great precision otherwise it may not be possible to acquire specified length and breadth. Moreover, the cutting may not be in a straight line thereby making the margins of the book look uneven. It is a common practice to trim a sample copy to see that blades of the machine are falling at the required points. Adjustments, to see that the edges are cut at right angle and printed lines are not in a slant, are made if necessary. The order of trimming should be fore edge first, followed by tail and head in the last. While cutting edges care is taken to achieve absolute squares.

## ROUNDING AND BACKING

Thickness of the back of each section increases after sewing. The spine, therefore swells and become, thicker than the fore edge side. The purpose of rounding is to remove any swelling in the back caused by sewing. The back of the book is first knocked flat covered with thin glue. Before the glue is completely dried, the back is tapped with a wooden or synthetic hammer until it is rounded and acquires a convex shape and fore edges take a concave shape.

After backing is done again with a hammer. The book is held between wedge shaped backing boards in a laying press. The back of the book is raised about 1/8" from it. Over the edge of these boards the back of the sections are tapped and fanned out evenly. The side sections are then hammered over on each side. Outside sections are beaten first followed by the more central sections. A groove is formed on both the sides.

As a result of tapping, edges of the joint become slightly higher than the total bulk of the book plus the thickness of the boards. The groove thus created is called French groove or French joint. The groove accommodates the covering material and facilitates the opening and closing of the book after binding without putting any pressure on the binding.

## LINING

Lining is sometimes attached to strengthen the paper, mull, leather or any other material so that binding can withstand the pressure caused by frequent and numerous opening and closing of a bound book. It also helps the book lie flat when opened. While lining up a coat of glue is applied to the spine and on it is placed a strip of cloth or guaze extending almost the length of the spine and about 1" over each side. Another coat of glue is applied on the guaze and a strip of strong paper cut to the size of the back is pasted on it. On heavier books stronger or double layer of guaze is applied. The extending portion of the guaze or mull is pasted on the board (cover) and beneath the end paper.

At this time headbands—a decorative strip of coloured cloth that protrude slightly at the back on top and bottom—are applied. These bands are placed in between the guaze and paper used in lining up a book. Headband is not only a decorative strip but also protects the book from insects getting inside the back of the book and also supports the head and tail of the spine.

## CASING IN AND ATTACHING THE BOARDS

The work of case making is done simultaneously with other operations discussed above. An efficient binder will not wait for the binding operations to reach the lining up stage to start working on case making. Since the dummy of the book provides details of measurements of the spine and other dimensions of the book, the work of preparing the case or cover is taken in hand alongwith other operations so that the case is ready by the time the book block is ready for casing in.

*Casing material:* The most commonly used materials for case making are boards for the cover on both sides, paper or pulp for the spine and from paper to plastic for the covering material. The qualities and varieties of materials for binding including cover are discussed separately in the following pages.

Case is the cover and backbone of a hard bound book. Also known as casing which is wrapped around and affixed to book's contents. The process of attaching the case to the book block is called casing in.

Cover boards are cut according to the size of the book. Boards should be cut according to the height of the book plus ¼" and width of the book less 1/8". By this way, when placed on each side it provides a projection of the size of 1/8" approximately.

This over hanging of the board beyond the book proper is called *squares.* Squares are projections of the boards beyond the edges of the leaves. Generally squares are kept as deep as the thickness of the board. Squares provide protection to the bound book from getting into direct contact with the surface while in use or storage. The back strip or spine is made slightly wider than the paper bulk or bulk of pages to allow swing or flare at the joint.

The covering material which may be paper, fabric rexine, leather is also cut 1¼" (3 cm) more than the height of the boards and 1¼" (3 cm) more than the width of the boards and back strip so that extra cover material is well folded and pasted back on the inside of the boards.

Case making can also be done on machines with precut pieces on sheet fed case maker or on a web fed case maker. The cover material and back strip paper is used in rolls.

In a sheet fed machine the material is glued on its inside surface, the boards and back strip are dropped on the wet glue in the proper position and small rollers push the turn is over and press them down to complete the cover.

In web fed case making machine, the material passes over a glue roller under a hopper which holds the boards. Back strip is mechanically cut off a roll and placed on to the glued material. Boards are also mechanically dropped in their respective position. As the web moves along the corners are cut to the required length and the edges are turned in.

## PASTING OF ENDPAPERS

The case is now complete ready to be attached to the book block. In casing in the book rides spine side up. It is at this stage end papers are applied to cover the inside of the cover board to give a smoother look.

Endpapers are two heavy leaves of thicker paper one at the beginning and the other at the end of the bound book connecting the covers to contents and function as hinges. One half of each leaf is pasted to the front and back cover. These are also called *End leaves* or *Fly leaves.*

Endpapers serve as a lining and cover the turn ins of the covering material. After the end papers covered with glue or adhesive are pasted, the whole book is squeezed together from both sides so that the glue sets in and binding becomes dry and durable.

## FAULTS OF BINDING

As we have seen there are several ways by which a book or document can be bound and each variety of binding style involves a certain number of operations. Unless a proper check is maintained on the stages through which a book passes during the process of binding one can not expect a desired quality of binding.

The common faults that appear in a carelessly done binding irrespective of its style are as follows:

1. *Careless* or *unimaginative folding*

As already discussed the printed sheets are first of all folded so that pages run in a continuous sequence. If folding to paper do not register the print on pages facing each other, folding should be done by the other method *i.e.* folding to print. This will avoid wrong alignment of running heads and provide uniform back margins which are sometimes difficult to achieve if folding is done carelessly or unimaginatively.

2. *Miscollation* or *Imperfection*

This is a very common fault in any kind of binding. This fault would creep in if collation is not properly checked by examining the collation marks on the back of the folded and gathered sheets. Any mis will result in either missing of a signature or duplicate signature instead. In both the cases it will be considered as imperfection and binder will be held responsible for that. Binder will not only loose money for the wrong binding but also looses reputation as a good binder.

3. *Sawing in*

The cuts derived with a saw to make sawing trenches across the back of the sections, should not be very deep. It should only be deep enough to fit the cord smugly. Deeper cuts will result in leaving projections in the back and ridges will be visible on the spine even after it is covered.

4. *Wire stapling*

In saddle stitch or side stitch binding styles the stitching is done by wire. The wire being much harder than the paper, the pages usually come off the stitches. The wire gets rusted in humid conditions and damage the paper and binding.

5. *Unsuitable adhesive*

In limp unsewn binding or perfect binding fast drying glue is applied on the spine of the book and later cover is attached to the book. As discussed earlier, in order to get the desired flexibility two shots of glue need to be applied. In tropical countries like India the binding which appears strong enough at the beginning become weak because the adhesive looses binding force and pages fall apart.

Adhesive reacts differently on different paper surface. Open and fibrous papers go very well with adhesive binding. If paper used in the book is of mixed quality and thickness, there is less likelyhood of glue sticking well for a long time. Such binding will remain weak. Extra care needs to be taken while trimming the three sides of the adhesive bound book. If trimming is not perfect the opposite pages will not be in one alignment.

6. *Glue Seepage*

In limp sewn or flexible binding nipping follows the sewing of sections. If nipping and smashing is not done properly and the back is not adequately flattened the glue will seep through from the back of the needle holes and pages stick together when book is opened. Seepage of glue also occurs because of inadequate lining. The same holds good for case binding also.

7. *Hollow back*

In a hollow back bound book space between the book block spine and inside of the case remains hollow. The covering material does not touch the spine and when the book is opened one could see down between the back of the book and back of the board. In hollow back the strain of opening is thrown over the joint and not distributed over the whole spine.

## MATERIALS FOR BINDING

The strength of binding largely depends upon the quality of binding material used. Binding materials and their choice will depend upon the kind of binding. The material used should be in commensurate with the durability and strength of paper of the book. If finances are any constraints and the book is to be sold at a cheaper rate one naturally cannot go in for expensive material. A finely printed book on good quality paper should necessarily have a strong and sturdy binding. On the other hand a cheaply produced popular fiction can be bound with inexpensive material. Similarly, different kinds of materials will be needed for different kinds of binding.

The material required and options available for hard cover binding are discussed below. Some of these raw materials are being chemically produced these days.

1. *Cover material*

Man has been using animal skins in olden days for covering the binding. As mass production of books started more cheaper and readily available materials were bound to be used as covering material. It includes cloth, synthetics, plastic paper etc. Commonly used covering materials are:

Leather
Cloth
Nonwoven material
Imitation cloth
Plastic coated paper
Paper

*Leather*

Leather is an ideal material for covering and protecting books. It has certain inherent qualities not found in any other material used for covering. It is soft, pliable, durable. It has natural strength and flexibility. Its surface is light and has natural fat or oil content that provides flexibility. It has qualities which no other covering material can boast of. The kinds of leather most commonly used in binding are:

(i) *Goat skin:* Goat skin also called Morocco is a common form of leather used. It has strongest network of grains. It is widely used in book binding since Renaissance times, though originating in North Africa, it is now made and used throughout the world. Even sheep skin is also sometimes converted into goat skin by using pressure mould taken out of goat skin.

(ii) *Calf Skin:* It is a soft variety of leather and it can be dyed easily to all shades. It is obtained from young animals.

(iii) *Sheep Skin:* It is weak and cheap leather which is not durable. Because of the weakness it is not recommended for reinforced library binding. Its surface is dull and porous and texture is loose which is not suitable for tooling in library binding.

(iv) *Seal:* It is very strong and rich leather with natural oil. Seal leather is very exquisite soft and beautiful. It is very expensive and rarely used because of nonavailability.

(v) *Vellum:* It is made of treated lamb or goat skin. After soaking the skin in limebath the hairs of the skin are removed. Vellum bindings are beautiful. The making of vellum is a time consuming process. It can be made into required thickness by scrapping.

(vi) *Miscellaneous skins:* Kangaroo skin, skins of snakes and reptiles, lizards and crocodiles have also been occasionally used as covering material for private collections.

(vii) *Bonded leather:* With the phenomenal increase in the book production figures in various parts of the world it became difficult and beyond reach to cover book binding with animal skins. The pressure gave a new byproduct of leather which looks like leather and is much less expensive. It is called bonded leather.

It is made up of pulp of different leather scraps. It is also called *reconstituted* leather. It consists of small leather particles compressed and bonded with a resin. It is available in rolls and is much cheaper than skins but costlier than cloth. It can be used for binding books of all kinds.

### *Cloth*

When leather is found too expensive woven fabric or cloth is used for covering material. Cloth for cover comes in a wide range of qualities, colours and finishes. Book cloth, binding cloth, calico, buckrum, mull, canvas and linen are some of the varieties used in binding of books.

Strength of the binding cloth depends upon the filler used in its manufacture. Most clothes are either filled with a composition consisting mainly of starch or plastic, usually pyroxylin or vinyle. Starch filled cloth is less durable and can not withstand dampness or moisture. Plastic filled cloth on the other hand is water resistant.

A good quality binding cloth should not stretch, should be reasonably water resistant and should have close texture. Loose textured cloth will allow adhesive to seep through and can spoil the binding.

Most commonly used binding clothes are as follows:

*Buckrum:* Very widely used binder's cloth is buckrum. It is a heavy and strong binder's cloth made from woven textile stiffened with size and available in several weights and finishes. Some common finishes are linen, vellum and natural in which dyed cloth is seen without the textural effect caused by filling.

*Mull or Muslin:* It is an open woven material used for lining the backs.

*Calico:* Cotton cloth used for front and back and not for the spine is also called calico.

No matter which variety of cloth is used for binding its capacity to receive the tooling and finishing should always be kept in mind while selecting.

*Nonwoven material*

It includes a class of synthetic cover material for book binding made from extrusion or felting rather than weaving. Nonwoven is also made from 100% synthetic fibre material and acrylic-reinforced cellulose. The high rising cloth price led to the use of nonwoven materials. These are much less costlier but give a much smoother look.

*Imitation cloth*

It is a reinforced paper which is dyed, optionally coated and then embossed with a range of patterns to imitate a number of cloth effects. It is available in a number of varieties depending upon their weight and the kind of treatment given to surface. Imitation cloth is available in rolls.

*Plastic coated paper*

Vinyl or PVC coated paper is available in wide variety of colours, surfaces and embossings. Vinyl or PVC coating provides thickness to the paper and also makes it water proof. The coating makes it suitable for machine use and also facilitates its gluing. The plastic coated paper is though a good substitute of leather, yet it is not problem free. Its faults include stretching, sticking together, repelling ink etc.

*Paper*

The most convenient and inexpensive cover material which is widely used by publishers and binders is the paper. It is available in various types of surfaces and body treatment. Paper made from craft paper with resin impregnation and a coating of lacquer or pyroxylin is strong enough to be used as trade book covers.

The other common type of paper used for cover material is dyed through with resin impregnation but without any coating. Also known as *Elephant Hide,* it has marble like appearance and has good strength, surface resistance to moisture.

Paper comes in less than the price of cheaper quality cloth and therefore widely used. Paper is also available in varieties of colour, weight and finish. Some are even embossed to give a special leather effect. Heavier variety of paper is also used as end papers.

2. *Boards*

The durability of hardcover binding largely depends upon the strength of the boards used for casing. If it breaks, cracks or warps, the binding will collapse. It is in the interest of strong binding that good quality board is used. Board is made mainly from recycled paper scraps, coarse cloth, ropes etc. Boards are made of varying thickness. Boards are generally available in the following varieties:

(i) *Chip board:* It is made from recycled newspaper, magazine waste. It is a poor quality binder's board that is weak and not used for standard books. It is inexpensive and, therefore, can be used when price dominates the quality. This board is grey in colour and also called unlined chip board.

(ii) *Straw board:* Originally the board used to be made from straw fibres. Now-a-days chip boards are occasionally lined with a yellow paper. Usually it is made from unbleached straw base pulp. It is less expensive but less durable also. It is, therefore, not recommended for strong binding.

(iii) *Pasted board:* In contrast to homogeneous board, pasted board is made from several layers of thinner sheets laminated together. By pasting a number of layers of chipboard pasted boards can be made of any thickness. This is the kind of board used for most of the books.

(iv) *Mill board:* Also known as Binder's board, it is made from solid sheets of rope fibres: Mill board is more expensive than the chip board. It is heavy, dense, hard and extremely rigid. It is made like paper and therefore does not warp or crack. It is most suitable for fine binding. The term mill board is sometimes used to denote normal case boards which are more properly grey boards or unlined chip boards.

*(v) Fibre board:* This is lighter in colour than mill board and is less expensive. This is used when stronger material is not considered necessary.

(vi) *Red board:* This a thin, tough, flexible board used for limp or flexible covers mainly of pocket looks. Boards are available in various sizes and colours.

### 3. *Endpaper*

Endpapers or fly leaves play a significant role in the strength of binding. The choice of end papers will depend upon the quality of paper used for printing of text. Endpapers bear the brunt of the strain when the book is opened or closed. End papers also serve as a link between the book block and the case.

A heavier book, therefore, would require end papers with good tensil strength. The paper used as endpaper is usually of a higher substance than the text paper. Some times self lining use of text paper as endpaper is also adopted. It may have the advantage of economy, but will not be able to accord extra strength because of the same substance of paper. The binding will remain weak.

Books with frequent and repeated use are not recommended self lining in endpapers. Endpapers are available in plain, coloured and marble finish. No matter what quality or surface is used for endpapers, care should be taken that they are pasted with grain direction, parallel to the spine.

### 4. *Tape*

Tapes are sewn along the spine to provide extra strength to the binding. The tape around which the thread is taken and against which the sheets are sewn should be of good quality unbleached linen. For books which are of permanent value, hampen cord is used instead of tapes.

### 5. *Thread*

If serves as a link in joining the various sections together. It has an important place among the materials and special care should be taken while selecting the thread—cotton or nylon thread can be used for sewing. Extra strong grades are available which can provide strength and durability to the binding.

Heavier cotton thread may create problem of bulking to the book back. Bleached cotton thread will be soft to handle but the process of bleach will weaken the strength of the thread. Unbleached cotton thread with required thickness should be used. Nylon thread is very thin and soft. It may not create problem of bulking but may cause slip pages if not properly tightened during the sewing process. Generally linen thread is used for section sewing. It is made of flex fibre, spun and waxed to give maximum strength.

6. *Adhesives*

Use of adhesive or glue is an important part of book binding process. In perfect binding the use of adhesive is the sole factor responsible for its strength or weakness. The choice of correct adhesive or glue for each specific operation is, therefore, very important. A general glue or adhesive may be useful for all operations where glue or adhesive is needed. The thickness and thinness of adhesive, its density, its drying time, power of penetration on application on materials, are some of the factors which need to be considered while choosing and applying any kind of adhesive.

The more common types of adhesives used in the process of binding are:

(i) *Paste:* It is made of vegetable starch, since it is prepared by flour, alum and water, it contains high moisture contents. It has a good penetration power. Paste is generally used for pasting paper to paper, board, leather etc., where drying is slow and is done by giving pressure. Slow drying properties allow the movement of paper after application of paste to avoid any wrinkles on the pasted surface.

(ii) *Gum:* It is made of exudation from trees. It has slow initial drying period and once applied and dried, sticks firmly. It is vulnerable to moisture.

(iii) *Glue:* Glue is used to paste cover material to boards and backing and lining of the spine in case binding and gluing of the back in perfect binding. Two types of glue are generally used.

*Scotch glue:* It is prepared from residual animal waste like bones, horns and skin. It is made in various forms of which the convenient is 'pearl' glue. It is made in granules which are dissolved in water and heated. It melts at low temperature and can be mixed readily with water and dries up very fast. It can be used where glue does not have to flex or fold. Because of the raw material used is animal waste it is also called *animal glue.*

*Flexible glue:* Flexible glue is again an animal glue which is made flexible by adding certain plasticised chemicals to prevent hardening. The special characteristic makes it most suitable for rounding and backing operations. It is also used on the spine of books where the movement is frequent. This glue also melts at low temperature. Because of its flexible properties it can be brushed on smoothly on the back or spine of the book.

(iv) *Synthetic adhesive:* Two types of synthetic adhesives are used in book binding.

*Polyvinyl Acetate Emulsions* (PVA): PVA is a water based synthetic adhesive. After drying it is formed into a thin transparent film of great flexibility. It is generally used in perfect binding.

*Hot melt:* This is also a type of synthetic resin adhesive used in perfect binding. Hot melt glue is solid at room temperature. It has high initial tack and dries quickly. Hot melt glue is a wax like substance of solid formation which is made from plasticised compound that is solid at room temperature but melts at more than 120°C.

When it melts, it becomes a very soft liquid which can be evenly applied on the back of the book and stiffens when temperature goes down. It sets quickly within seconds and is most suitable for perfect binding when the glue is applied with the binding machine.

### 7. *Headbands*

Headband is a cotton or silk cord attached to the top and bottom edge of the book spine of a hard bound book. The purpose of headband is to provide beauty and durability to the binding. Headbands have rolled edges and are woven one solid colour or pattern of alternative stripes.

## GLOSSARY OF BINDING TERMS

*Attaching:* Joining the boards to the main sections of a book with a French joint or to a tight joint.

*Back lining:* The gluing of lining material to the inside of the backbone of a book during binding. The pages of the book, in signatures, are glued to the lining and air space is left between lining and backbone, also called backing.

*Beating:* Hammering the folded sections to lie flat.

*Case:* Cover of the book bulk made by hand or machine consisting of boards. A hollow binding material. The case is attached to the book block. Also called *casing in* or *case binding.*

*Collating:* Checking of the signatures of a book to determine its completeness and correctness of sequence.

*Collation marks:* Small marks printed at certain place on the sheets so that when folded each signature will have one along its back edge. The marks are printed in a step style so that a diagonal line across the back appears when the book is gathered in orderly sequence. Any error becomes, apparent looking at the collation marks of gathered signatures of a book.

*Endpapers:* The papers pasted to the inside of the front and back covers of a casebound book. Also called end leaves or fly leaves.

*Finishing:* Lettering and decoration on a cover of a book including spine. It includes operations occurring after the book is put together such as ornamenting, etc.

*Flexible Binding:* A kind of binding in which the binder's boards are made of flexible material and resulting covers are flexible. Also called limp binding.

*Flexible glue:* A kind of glue which contains a substance that prevents it from drying out completely. Usually used for g1uing the back of the book after sewing.

*Flyleaf:* Same as end papers. Sometimes a name given to any blank leaf at the front or back of a publication including the endpapers.

*Forwarding:* A generic name for operations of binding a book after the sheets are sewn together. It includes trimming, gluing, rounding, backing, attaching the board and covering. All operations after sewing and before finishing.

*French Joint:* A depression between the board and the book. Usually used in library binding. When boards are placed on the book so that a square projects at the fore edge; a French groove equal in measurement to the square will be formed at the joint; also called *French Groove.*

*Gathering:* Assembling the sheets of a book in an orderly sequence.

*Guards:* Folded strips of paper sewn or pasted in the back of the book.

*Headband:* Decorative band at the top and also at the bottom of the spine of a book intended to take the strain of a user's finger as a book is removed from the shelf.

*Hollow:* Spine of the hard cover book which creates a space between the backbone of the book and the back of the book's contents, so that the book will lie flat when opened.

*Kettle Stitch:* A chain stitch of the sewing in which thread is carried up and down across the entire back of the book linking the sections at head and tail.

*Mull:* Thin woven fabric used to line the spine.

*Sawing in:* Grooves made at the back of the collated book with a saw to receive the thread for binding.

*Section:* A folded sheet.

*Sheet:* Open full size sheet before folding into folios or Quarto subdivisions. A broadside or open sheet.

*Signature:* A sheet of a book as folded ready for sewing. The size of book will determine the number of folds. To make a 16 page signature from a sheet with 8 pages on each side, 3 right angle folds are needed.

*Slips:* The end of the tapes or cords that are attached to the cover boards during binding.

*Spine:* The part of a book binding visible when the book stands vertical on the shelf. Part of the casing of a book which connects the front and back covers.

*Square:* Projections of the boards beyond the edges of the leaves.

No matter what kind of binding has been chosen and what material used after a book is bound it is ready to be sent to the publisher's warehouse and from this moment onwards sales and promotion section takes charge of the publication.

# Part IV
# Promotion and Sales—Selling the Book

# 19

# Sales Promotion Methods

Some publishers have separate sales promotion department while other austre ones; leave sales and promotion to persons with undefined job description in the publishing house. It is, therefore, necessary to know clearly what is sales promotion and what, role does it play in the successful performance of a book and thereby sustaining the publishing activity of a publishing house.

## SALES PROMOTION

Sales promotion can be defined as activity which consists of marketing of a product or promotion of a service. It includes functions such as personal selling, advertising, displays, exhibitions and other activities which increase sales and expand the market of a product.

Sales promotion aims to provide direct stimulus to produce a desired response by customers. It is also defined as a 'direct inducement which offers an extra value or incentive for the product to sales force, distributors or the ultimate consumer'. In our context the product which is pushed forward for sales is the book.

Sales promotion consists of certain materials and techniques which are used to help sell the product. Sales promotion materials are usually not directly aimed at the actual buyer by the publisher, but are prepared for the use of the retail seller. Sales promotion is diverse collection of incentive tools, mostly of short term nature designed to stimulate quicker or greater purchase of a particular product by the actual user or the trader.

In the context of book publishing promotion consists of all the methods used by a publisher to inform the world about the existence of a book and persuade and prompting the people to buy it.

*Objectives of Sales Promotion:* Promotion is done to achieve the following objectives:

1. To attract new customers.
2. To reward loyal customers.
3. To get results faster than advertisement.
4. To combine it with advertisement to get higher/quicker yield of customers.

The consumer, the trade and the sales force is kept in mind while preparing sales promotion for a product. Tools of consumer promotion such as samples, coupons, cash refund offers, discounts, prizes, patronage awards, free gifts etc. are used in book promotion also. Trade promotion tools may include buying allowance, free goods delivery, sale or return facility, cooperative advertising, display allowances, push money incentives and dealers, sale contest. Sales force promotion sometimes include bonuses, contests, promotions, incentives etc. A combination of these tools is usually employed by a publisher to promote a book. Sales promotion department of a publishing house prepares marketing plan for each book that is published.

## SALES PROMOTION PLAN

Each book is different and, therefore, promotion needs for each book will also be different. In developing a sales promotion plan or marketing strategy the most important component in the entire process of book promotion is the book itself. The strategy to promote and sell a desired number of copies will depend upon (1) the nature of the book, and (2) the corresponding market. Since promotion budget is always inadequate, the promotion manager has to be judicious in the choice of methods which are applied to get the desired results.

A promotion plan should be designed to achieve the highest sale potential of the book. A wisely thought of marketing compaign can achieve upto 80 to 90 percent of target sales where a poor marketing effort would achieve only 20 to 25 percent of target sales.

The time and energy spent in advance planning and developing a suitable marketing plan for individual book will bring in more sales and profit, the lack of it will result in slow sales and no profit.

It is generally said that charity begins at home. So is book promotion. The information about the new book, before it goes out in the market, is spread first within the publishing house. This may also be termed as internal promotion. The event which triggers the process of selling books and serves as the basis of internal promotion within the publishing house is called the sales conference.

*Sales conference:* In publishing language sales conference is also known as concept meeting or advance meeting. In medium size publishing house such meetings are held twice or three times a year depending upon the number of titles being published by publishing house. Though the timings of the conference would differ from publisher to publisher, yet most conveniently these are held at the middle or the end of the year.

The agenda of the sales conference would normally be:

(i) To introduce new and forthcoming titles.
(ii) To initiate promotion techniques.
(iii) To outline advertisement and publicity plans.
(iv) To announce special packages or discounts to attract higher/quicker sales.
(v) To spell out the markets for the books.
(vi) To fix sale quota, if necessary, for the sales staff.
(vii) To provide dust jackets, circular letters and other pieces of printed information.
(viii) To take stock of selling position of back list and current list titles and other related topics.

*Who attends the sales conference:* The sales conference is attended by sales and promotion manager, sales staff including field representatives, staff dealing with advertising and publicity and persons looking after the subsidiary rights and persons from the accounts branch. Editor of the book is the most indispensable participant because it is the editor who introduces the title to the conference audience. The conference may last a couple of hours or days depending upon the number of titles being introduced in the meeting.

*Proceedings:* Sales manager generally presides over the meeting and editor plays the part of the chief speaker. The editor introduces each title giving information about the author, title, subject coverage and other plus points of the title and also explains the possible markets for a title.

The main listeners are the sales staff. They are encouraged to ask questions about the books. Some of the essential details about the titles is provided on separate sheets which may either be typed or printed.

This information sheet is usually called advance notice/sheet. This sheet would provide information about the author, title, brief description of the contents, possible competitive titles and production details etc. The format of the advance sheet would more or less be as follows:

PUBLISHING HOUSE
ADVANCE SHEET

Title
Author(s) / Editor(s)
Address (optional)
Subject
Contents (Brief description)
Comparative titles
Other books by the author
Highlights of the book
Market
Production details:

| | |
|---|---|
| Book size | Number of pages |
| Publication date | Expected price |

Quota for sales staff (optional)
(Any other information)

Only precise and concise information is given about each title. Details are avoided. The idea is to make them aware of the highlights of the books and not to confuse them with more details.

The editor's introduction is followed by the information about publicity and advertisement compaign for the titles introduced. Sale performance of previously published books is also sometimes reviewed and assessed.

The meeting usually ends with fixing up sale quotas by the sales manager so that each salesman knows his target and efforts, one is supposed to put in for achieving the desired target. Field staff is also provided with materials which have been prepared for point of purchase publicity and other mailing materials like catalogues, posters etc.

The conference provides the field staff a thrust to meet the challenge of sale target, keeps the back list sale going and also enables the field staff to serve as a liaison between the publisher and the market to provide a feed back on the effectiveness of the sales promotion plan for a title.

## PROMOTION METHODS

There are as many ways of promoting a title as there are titles to promote. There are certain methods of book promotion which are basic and fundamental to all kinds of books produced while there ate others, which are optional, which may be used or applied keeping in mind the nature of the book, availability of budget and other related factors.

For successful sales promotion programme, the sales manager must establish the objectives, select the most suitable methods of promotion, develop a well organised programme, implement it, control and evaluate it.

Any book promotion plan will keep the potential market in view while finalising the strategy. The word 'market' includes the following three areas of possible sale:

Trade
Institutions
Individuals

For every book published there would be trade outlets, wholesalers, retailers and specialised booksellers, institutions doing teaching and, research work in that specific area or discipline and individuals pursuing studies in that area of knowledge.

A model promotion plan would, therefore, adopt a strategy that will cover all the three segments of a market. This may include directing promotion methods in the following areas:

1. Point-of-purchase publicity
2. Materials for Mailing
3. Advertisement
4. Author's participation
5. Book reviews
6. Utilisation of sales force
7. Other miscellaneous methods

1. *Point-of-purchase publicity*

Point of purchase is retail book store from where a book can be purchased. It is the most suitable place to make the presence of the book felt by way of displays. In other consumer products like soaps, shampoos and chocolates, the retail store is flooded with creative and attractive point of purchase display materials to attract the attention of the potential buyers. The idea is to remind the presence of the stocks.

In book industry the competition is not as fierce as in other consumer products. Since the availability of space in a bookshop is always scarce, the display material should be designed in such a way that without occupying more space it should prominently display the message—the title or jacket of the book.

The point of purchase displays are promotional items that are designed to sell books in and out side the store. It includes items like (i) posters or hangers, (ii) window stickers, (iii) display racks and (iv) pre packs and such other materials which can provide extra handle to the books and offer the buyers an incentive for buying.

(i) *Posters/Hangers:* These are usually made of card board, pulp paper or art paper sheets, printed generally on one side only and meant for vertical display. The poster may have the book jacket .or title prominently printed. These posters become identification device and remind the customers of the presence of the title and help them to identify it. The improved processes and techniques have made it possible to prepare colourful and attractive posters at fairly low cost. The posters are also used as mailing material.

(ii) *Window Stickers or Streamers:* With the development of imported adhesives and printing techniques it has become possible to produce self adhesive stickers or streamers at a relatively low price. These are much smaller in size than posters and hangers and used in bookstore display windows and other display areas in a bookshop.

(iii) *Display racks or Wire racks:* As part of promotion plan a tie up can be done with a bookstore by providing him a wooden rack or wire rack on the understanding that for a certain period of time the bookstore will display publisher's title(s) and after the expiry of time agreed upon, the rack may be retained by the book seller for its use. The purpose of this kind of arrangement is to provide prominent display to books and giving them an edge over other books lying in the bookstore.

(iv) *Pre-packs:* It means special packaging of books before they reach the point of sale. Pre-packed books may contain a gift coupon or some other attractive offer for the buyer. Sometimes pre-packed books may have special kind of binding in order to attract customers.

These are not the only items of point of purchase display. Imagination and alertness of the promotion manager can create so many other things subject to budget available for promotion. Bookmarks, display buttons and such other materials are used to influence the customers. Many publishers, these days, pay a lot of attention to point of purchase display materials as they have become increasingly important to attract the attention of impulse purchase.

Even though books do not come under impulse purchase category of goods but visibility is of crucial importance. The more innovative the display at the bookstore, the greater are the chances of getting noticed and finally picked up by the purchaser.

2. *Materials for mailing*

Promotion of books through mail or post is an important component of the composite promotion policy of a publishing house. This is done to promote and publicise the books. A variety of mailing materials in various shapes and forms is mailed out to wholesalers, retailers, institutions and individual buyers. The material for mailing would depend upon the promotion budget and size of the potential market.

Publishers use a variety of materials for mailing. Most commonly used materials for mailing include:

Jacket
Trade Announcements and circular letters
Brochure
Catalogues and publisher's lists

*Jacket:* Jacket is the printed outer cover 'placed over the binding of a hard cover book which provides space for visual display. It contains the name of the author, title of the book and usually designed carefully to be eye catching and to serve as an identification device to recognise a book. The back of the jacket and inner flaps are used as promotional copy (also called blurb). It is also called dust jacket or dust cover.

The jacket is used as publicity material and sent sometimes in advance of publication of the book to various trade outlets and institutions and libraries. The back of the jacket and inner flaps provide enough space to write something about the author and the book to enhance its marketability

*Trade announcements and circular letters:* In order to provide information to the trade about the new titles, their publication date, price and incentives, if any, publishers use circular letters or trade announcements. These are not items of individual promotion but are used alongwith other mailing materials like monthly bulletin or brochures etc.

Such circulars are sent to wholesalers and retailers in quantity so that they can send these to their customers or as part of their mailing. Such circulars are also carried by sales staff when they visit the market for sale and promotion of the books.

*Brochure:* A brochure is a booklet devoted to advertising matter, often illustrated and using good deal of display type. A brochure can be simple as well as very attractive. Brochures may vary in size and shape ranging from a small folded broad side sheet to substantial booklet or even a small book.

Brochures may contain in brief, salient features of the book. Since each book will have different subject, approach and audience, each brochure has to be designed separately and differently, keeping in mind the readership. Time factor in such publicity is of prime factor. A late or delayed attempt may not give the desired results.

While writing for the brochure one should keep the target audience and potential users in mind. A brief description of the contents of the book may be followed by the mechanical features *i.e.* the size and number of pages etc. The copy should include information about the subject and author of the book.

Not all books would need brochures for their publicity. But if the subject is topical and readership is wide and identified such material for mailing can also be tried within budgetary limitations.

*Catalogues and publishers' lists:* A catalogue is a list of books published by a publishing house systematically arranged either by author or subject with descriptive information prepared for a specific purpose of sales and promotion. Depending upon the number of books published by a publishing house a catalogue is published once, twice or more times in a year. It is also called publisher's list.

It contains information about the books already published, books in press and books to be published in a near future. A catalogue serves as a ready reckoner of a publisher's publishing programme. These catalogues are also mailed to the trade, institutions and libraries and potential buyers of publisher's books.

*Mailing list:* The success and failure of mailing programme depends upon the effectiveness of publisher's mailing list. A mailing list is a list of names and addresses compiled by interest of activity of trade customers, institutions and individual consumers. The compilation of list requires careful consideration of the audiences and groups that will use and benefit from the book or books offered.

Brochures and other mailing materials are mailed to the prospective buyers. Sending publicity material though mailing list is a direct method of advertising which can be used very effectively if the list of names and addresses is compiled carefully and kept constantly updated.

For every book published there would be following categories of buyers.

Trade
Institutions
Individuals

*Trade:* Booksellers' directories and other such publications of professional associations will provide information about booksellers and wholesalers in a given area or city. Their names can be included is the mailing list. It is not enough to know the name of the bookseller or wholesalers but also the nature of books sold by them and also their credit worthiness. If these things are ignored the list may not give the desired results in helping the sale of the book.

*Institutions:* Associations and organisations are composed of individuals with a common interest or common bond. The aim of such organisations and institutions is to provide certain services to their members. Selling books may not be the aim of such organisations but buying books and providing access to their members may be a function which most organisations perform.

Libraries, corporate offices, professional organisations and academic associations fall in the category of institutions for the purpose of preparing a mailing list by publishing house. Since each organisation or association is catering to the specific interests of its members, the inclusion in the mailing list should be carefully done so that the promotion efforts do not go waste.

*Individuals:* This a very wide area of mailing list. There may be individuals, lecturers, professors, government officials, librarians and all such persons who can directly and individually influence the sale of a book. For each book there would be a separate set of individuals included in the list. For example a professor of history may not find a place in a mailing list prepared for a text book on physics. But a librarian may in both the lists.

Mailing list for each book may be different depending upon the factors like prospective buyer's age, sex, income, lifestyle etc. while preparing the mailing list one should identify the publication with interest and needs of the book's potential audiences.

Drawing up a mailing list should be done with a sense of discrimination. Because undistinguished list would cost a lot of money without achieving any worthwhile results.

3. *Advertisement*

Every publisher would do some sort of advertising for every book that is published. Advertisement of some sort is an obligation on the part of the publisher. How much advertisement is needed to promote a given title would depend upon the nature of the book, the nature of the potential buyers and number of copies printed and amount of budget available for the purpose.

Advertisement is a very costly way of promoting a book. Therefore, it should be used very cautiously. Advertisement is necessary (alongwith other methods) to get the book to the target audience and also to make the retailers and other trade market aware of the product. It also has certain advantages in book promotion plan. It provides and appeal to the trade, the bookstore and individual buyers. It also has an influence on the sale of the subsidiary rights.

For authors, advertisement is a tool to project their image. If their book is not advertised, they sometimes believe that publisher is not promoting the book properly. Advertising is a costly affair. What authors do not realise that the cost of quarter page or half page of advertisement in a popular magazine or a newspaper is sometimes equal to the total book budget. Moreover, people read newspapers and magazines for their news value and not advertisement value. Publishers should, therefore, be the best judge as to which book should be advertised and where. Normally a publisher allocates approximately 10% of the anticipated net sales in a year and then decides which title should be advertised prominently.

Does advertisement sell books? Opinion vary on the effectiveness of book advertising. Max Perkins, the celebrated editor (of Scribner) compared advertising a book to the problem of a car that is stuck. He believed thus. "If a car is really stuck in the mud, then people can't budget it. But if it is moving a little bit one man can push it down the road. By the same token, if the book is absolutely dead, all advertisement in the world isn't going to help. If it is got glimmer of life, it is selling a little bit may be in one or two, it is moving enough to give a push."

Every book need not be advertised in the press. There are books which can sell more by direct point to point sale if the market is identified. Still advertisement in major national newspapers is generally most effective for books of wider appeal.

Television is another medium of advertisement. But even television advertisement is also very costly. Radio advertisement on the other hand, is cheaper. Options such as coupon advertisement where coupon printed in the advertisement can be used by a potential buyer for some concession or special rebate is another form where books can be advertised.

Because of prohibitive cost group advertisement combining several titles or cooperative advertisement associating another bookselling agency or some other body is also used as another option to minimise the cost of advertisement.

Though some publishers feel that other methods aggressively followed can compensate the need for advertising still the results of book advertisement as a method of promotion is worth the money spent on it.

4. *Author's Participation*

Publishing is a business where author occupies the centre stage position. Author's role in book promotion can not be under estimated. Author's care as well as utilisation of author's resources are an integral part of publishing and promotion of books. As every author wants publicity, he can also provide publicity to the publishing house.

There are many areas of book promotion where author can playa significant role. Author's participation and the methods used for the same would largely depend upon the nature of the book and the status of the author. The areas where author can contribute in book promotion include:

(i) Letters
(ii) Tours
(iii) Autograph sessions
(iv) Interviews
(v) Subsidiary rights selection and sale
(vi) Selection of review media
(vii) Personal connections

(i) *Letters:* Publisher should not forget that the author writes. Not only that the author has written a book, can also write additional pieces of interest of the topic of the book. Author's views on the subject may be arranged to be published in newspapers and magazines. By this way the book is promoted indirectly. Not only that, an author is the best judge because of his intimate knowledge of the subject as to what kind of people and groups would be interested in the book and which professional associations care about the subject.

The author would know whether the book will be valuable as text book or supplementary reading in schools and colleges. Author may be asked to draft letters highlighting the relevant area of the book and the same may be sent to educational institutions. Author's letters can also accompany other publicity material and promotional literature prepared by the publisher for mailing.

(ii) *Author's tour:* For trade books and general fiction, author's tour can be major marketing tool for the publisher. It may, though, have limited appeal for works of professional and scholarly nature. If your author has made a major scientific break through or is a noted celebrity in the field of literature or any other area of popular appeal and has the ability of interpersonal communication, such an author can play a great role by organising tours and talking about the book.

Such tours are generally planned in advance and tied up with local booksellers to provide extra discount and proper display during the author's personal appearance at the event site. In the beginning, tours canbe undertaken on experimental basis. If the response is good and encouraging such tours can be extended to other areas.

One of the greatest success story in contemporary publishing is traceable to series of talks initiated by a lesser known author. The book *I am OK You're OK,* had an advance sale of 7433 copies and sold 19843 copies during the first year. Sales went upto 100,000 in the next year and continued to mount until they peaked at over a million in 1973.

Stuart Harris, publicity director of Harper and Row gives credit to the author Thomas A. Harris because his talks before small audiences got sales to a point where publicity department felt justified in planning a strong promotional plan which included author's tours.

In Indian context their have been some examples where authors contributed to the high volume sale of their books.

Larry Collins and Dominique Lapaire, Kuldeep Nayar, Kusum Sawhney and Bejan Daruwala are a few names which deserve mention.

(iii) *Autograph sessions:* Closely related to author's discussions and tours are autograph sessions. These can be arranged only if the author is a celebrity and people can easily recognise him/her. There have been many examples where well known figures in public life have given autograph sessions where they personally autograph the books purchased at the site. Publishers have used this method of book promotion successfully when authors like Khushwant Singh, Kiran Bedi, Kapil Dev, Bejan Daruwala obliged individual customers with their autographs on the books they purchased on that occasion.

(iv) *Author's Interviews:* Besides, autograph sessions at designated sale points, author's appearance on radio, television or interview in a major newspaper or journal provides free publicity which generates sales. This can cover up the deficiency of book advertisement. Such appearance on radio and television and through press is a very effective tool for reaching the potential readers. Care should be taken that subject matter of the book should have sufficient mass appeal to warrant exclusive media coverage.

(v) *Subsidiary Rights:* Sale of subsidiary rights to book clubs and paper back publishing houses sometimes make the publishing of a title economically viable. Income from such sources sometimes exceeds the income from the sale of original edition. Authors tan certainly help the publishers in such sales. Intimate knowledge of the subject can make the difference between getting offers and getting ignored. Author can suggest which chapter of the book can be used as excerpts in which magazine or newspaper. Authors can help the publisher in pinpointing the areas which can be exploited for sale of subsidiary rights.

(vi) *Review Copies:* As a matter of policy, most publishers send copies of every new book to major review media. The review media that caters to a large audience also pay attention to serious books that may not have mass appeal. The impact of book review would depend upon the kind of book reviewed and the media in which the review appears.

Some professional journal may not have vast readership, can print effective reviews. The promotion department of a publishing house may not have exact idea of such professional journals. Authors can be of great help in drawing up a review media list which may include small town papers and other professional journals which are devoted to the specific subject area of the book.

More information on book review as method of book promotion is given separately in the following pages.

(vii) *Personal Connections:* Personal connections of the author also play a vital role in promoting and selling the book. If the author has good acquaintances with professionals, teachers, research scholars, librarians and men of literary merit, the same can be used for promoting a title. Author's close liaison with such people can greatly help the promotion efforts of the publisher.

5. *Book review*

For every book published there would be a potential review media—newspapers, magazines, journals etc. which may alongwith other literature on the subject of the book may carry review pages. A wise promotion manager would maintain a file of review policies and practices of various newspapers and journals to which copies of the books may be sent for reviewing. This is important because getting a book reviewed in a journal totally unrelated to the subject of the book may do more harm than good.

Reviews are vital far successful selling of professional and scholarly books. Review media help to reach the potential market. As discussed in the earlier paragraphs, author's help should be sought in identifying the right review media.

How many copies should be sent for review would differ from book to book. The following factors play a great role in deciding how many copies should be sent for reviewing:

Size of the country

Language of the book

Number of review media

Coverage of the book

Nature of the book

Size of the edition

Usually 10% of the edition is set aside for review and presentation.

Practice varies from publisher to publisher regarding reminding the newspaper/magazine editors about reviews. Pestering the review editors to publish reviews is not advisable. This kind of chasing the reviewer may prove counter productive. What is needed that if a magazine is not responsive to your books, which you may have sent over a period of time, you may drop that newspaper or magazine rather than asking questions. Authors can be most persuasive for such a follow up as most authors tend to know newspaper/magazine editors on personal terms. A proper record of reviews published should be maintained as these excerpts may be used in other promotional literature.

Book reviews carry a lot of weight in decision making in the institutional book purchase. A librarian may be influenced more by a small piece of book review than a prominent advertisement. Book reviews can be mailed to institutions with other mailing material. A book review, therefore, has a multiplier effect and can be used as public relations tool with the author. Sending a copy of the review to the author would serve two purposes.

(i) The author would feel grateful for the interest you are taking in the promotion of the title.

(ii) If the media has been recommended by the author, it will give a feeling of confidence in the publisher that his suggestion has been respected. Author will, willingly join hands with the publisher in his efforts to promote the title.

Whether or not a book should be advertised in the issue in which the review is appearing is a debatable point. It would be safer to avoid advertising in the same issue. If you must, insert your advertisement in the following issue so that the advertisement can have double effect, review being fresh in the minds of the readers.

Some newspapers and magazines publish a list of books received far reviewing. Mere listing evokes some interest and generates query which sometimes results into sale orders. Publication of book reviews also provide word of mouth publicity and help in book sale.

There is also a practice to send advance copies for review to coincide, preferably with the date of release of the book. In such a case as soon as the galleys are ready or page proofs are ready, one set is sent as advance copy for review. Sometimes bound galleys are sent as advance copy.

This practice is not without its pitfalls. If the review is good a publisher can hope a faster sale of the title. A negative review may mar the chances of brisk sale after the book is released. If the review is good excerpts from it can be used as blurb on the jacket or can be used in the copy for advertisement and other promotional material.

No matter whether the book is reviewed before publication date or after, a wise use of book review can be the least expensive and most effective method of book promotion.

6. *Utilisation of Sales Force*

For publishers, the sales representatives constitute their sales force. Their is no substitute to utilisation of sales force for selling books by the publishers. All other promotional methods can achieve the desired results only if the sales staff is covering the market.

As already discussed in the earlier pages the agenda of sales conference is always to inform and familiarise the sales force about the new and forthcoming books, providing them the promotional materials likes brochures, catalogues, posters, jackets etc., and informing them the sales promotion plan for a book or set of books. Sometimes target of sales is also given to the sales force.

Sales staff serves the following useful purposes:

1. It helps the publisher to sell larger number of copies of a title.

2. It also carries back information about the titles already published (back list); how these titles are selling in market. Whether there is any more demand for these books.
3. It also provides a feedback about publicity efforts made by the publisher and helps redirecting or repositioning the promotional efforts.
4. It also serves as public relations department of the publishing house as it can provide information about the publishing programmes and policies.
5. It also suggests the areas where the book is fairing well and the areas where promotional efforts need to be strengthened.
6. It can also help finalising arrangements for cooperative advertising with retailers.
7. It would also inform the bookstores, wholesalers and institutions about forthcoming publications and any special incentives which can be offered on selected new and back list titles.
8. It may also finalise the arrangements of an author's appearance for autograph session at a particular bookstore.
9. The feed back from the sales staff in the form of reports provide an overview of the publisher's efforts regarding success or failure of promotional efforts.

There is, therefore, no substitute to the use of sales force in the implementation of book promotion plan.

### 7. *Other Miscellaneous Methods*

It is generally said that there are as many ways of promoting a title as there are titles to promote. What is required is the imagination of the promotion manager and pulling the right cord. The list of methods which can be and have been tried is endless. From cinema slides to paper caps anything can be used as promotion tool. From book events to stunts and gimmicks, anything can be tried that is suitable to your kind of books. Some more commonly used miscellaneous methods are:

*(i) Exhibitions:* The organisation of exhibitions of any product(s) for demonstrating quality and service to the consumers is becoming very popular these days for special sale appeal. In such exhibitions products are demonstrated and sold at special discount to the customers.

In the same fashion books can also be promoted and sold through exhibitions. The participation in an exhibition provides the potential buyers an opportunity to handle the books and see the contents etc., before actually buying them. Books are sold directly to customers or orders may be procured to deliver the books at a later date. When an event of this kind is arranged invitations are sent to potential buyers and the event is also advertised and special discounts are offered to attract more visitors.

*(ii) Sample/Specimen Copies:* Specimen or sample copies, different from review copies are sent to people who may directly or indirectly influence the sale of the book. These copies are sent to professors, and lecturers in University and colleges, school teachers, administrators and people in position who may help in popularising the book. Sometimes authors also provide a list of persons whom such copies may be sent. The list should be followed with caution because in many cases it may only include the names of author's friends.

*(iii) Launching party:* Launching an author or book is an ideal public relation event. There should be a rational, reason for such a party. In such a party, reviewers and members of the press are invited. Copies of the book are displayed. Teachers and professors are also invited to such launching parties. It is basically a publicity event which involves a lot of money. Only such authors and books which are newsworthy should be launched at such events.

*(iv) Book release function:* Book release function, apart from launching party is an other important promotion method. Important books are released at a well organised function where a prominent figure in the subject area is asked to speak a few words on the author and his work and the book is released to the public. The audience for such function consists of university teachers, administrators, traders and potential buyers of the book. The function, if properly organised gets free publicity in the press because press is also invited for the coverage of the function.

*(v) Radio and Television:* Radio and television can provide a big boost to book promotion and booksale. There are a number of radio and TV programmes which discuss books and authors. Authors appearance can be of great help in popularising the book. A television programme interviewing the author and introducing the subject of the

book to the viewers can be a great booster of book sale. Not all authors and books can be promoted on radio and television. Authors with quick thinking and articulate knowledge should be exposed to this kind of promotional method.

*(vi) Participation in Book Fairs:* The primary objective of book fairs has been to foster book mindedness and to promote the growth of publishing. Participation in book fair of national and international level gives an opportunity to expose the product to lakhs of people who visit the book fair. Book fairs help to keep abreast of the latest publications in the country and in the world. They also serve as a meeting place for authors, publishers and librarians and the readers. The fairs bring all the potential readers to a platform where books from hundreds of publisher are displayed. The fairs are great national and international events. Participation in such fairs is eagerly awaited by most publishers.

The basic purpose of book promotion is to bring author's work in public attention. A successful promotion may depend upon the conventional methods but the ability to carve out new ideas to project the title is key to successful book promotion. A promotion manager will not be tied up with the conventional approaches but continue to seek, to find new areas of experimentation to bring profits to the publisher and satisfaction to the author.

# 20

# Book Club

Bookselling through mail order has undefined boundries. Another logical extension of mail order selling is the institution of book clubs, which may be operated independently or an organ of a publishing house.

Book club can be defined as a membership organisation functioning as a vehicle for the sale and distribution of books to its members, periodically, usually monthly, offering for sale books as main selections, which members may purchase or reject.

The idea of book club has not caught up in India in a big way, though there are a few book clubs operating in this country. In other countries book club sales have made significant contribution to the publishers' profit. In India we do not have large number of bookshops. It is difficult to buy a book if you are located in an area which is away from metro cities. People do not have access to books except at all through libraries which again are few and far between.

The business of book club is guided by two basic principles. (i) The price per copy can be reduced substantially by increasing the print run. (ii) That there are hundreds and thousands of potential buyers who could not be served by the traditional bookshops. Some mechanism, therefore, is needed to tap the unexplored market which exists in great abundance.

This mechanism is found in reaching the potential market through post, sending books by mail and receiving the payment in return through mail. The success of this machanism depends upon a well established and dependable mail or postal system.

In U.S.A and U.K. book clubs exist today for almost every kind of reading. Subjects selected for sale through book clubs include general books, cook books, books on philosophy, self development, how to do books, biographies, serious fiction and juvenile literature.

Book club is like a personal bookstore where by sitting at home one gets a list of books available in the book club catalogue. The idea is very attractive for many potential buyers, who could not otherwise make it to a bookshop to buy a book of their choice. Book clubs inform the potential buyers, through their catalogues and other mailing materials, which new titles have been published and what they are all about. In general, information about the new books is as scarce as the books themselves. Moreover, books are offered at the fraction of the price of the original edition.

## STRUCTURE OF A BOOK CLUB

A book club is like a publishing house with editorial, production, marketing and order fulfilment as their main functions or departments. The entire process is monitored by the management board.

*Editorial:* Certain book clubs have independent editorial board which makes selection of titles from galleys or bound books submitted to them by the original publishers. The editors negotiate subsidiary rights with the publishers and finalise the titles to be included as a book club selection or edition.

Depending upon the nature of the book, publishers sometimes submit their manuscript for book club option to more than one club simultaneously. In such a situation the club has to make a bid for the same. The amount offered by book clubs to the main publisher differs from book to book and club to club.

The guiding principles for the book club would include the subject area, reputation of the author, promotion budget of the publisher of the original edition. The possible price difference between the original and book club edition and above all the hunch of the editorial board. Keeping in view the unpredictable nature of publishing business, no success is guaranteed.

The negotiation for a title would normally include the advance guarantee amount, schedule of payment, rate of royalty, liability of the book club and the territory in which the club is authorised to sell to its members.

*Production:* After the deal has been finalised, the responsibility of producing the book or looking after the production work, production of mailing material for the club members falls on the production department. This may include production of the club edition, printing of extra copies simultaneously with the publisher or lifting stocks from the publisher.

*Promotion and Marketing:* The job of promoting and marketing the book club titles occupies the centre stage in the operations of a book club. Promotion department employs copy writers to write convincing and persuasive letters to subscriber members and to the new subscribers to be. Book club promotion also includes writing circular letters, announcements, press advertisements, preparation of brochures, catalogues and news bulletins.

The success, and failure of the book club promotion depends upon the persuasive copy writing. Great attention, therefore, is given to the copy and layout of the material designed by mailing.

*Order Fulfilment:* This section keeps a track of the membership list, mailing of the ordered books, keeping a strict time schedule for each job. Another important job of the section is to provide a feedback regarding effectiveness of the promotional campaign. It also looks after the incoming mail which will include orders, queries, reminders and also complaints.

## BOOK CLUB OPERATIONS

A book club's mainstay are the subscribers, who have agreed to purchase a certain number of titles in a year. The number may be three or four titles or more depending upon the requirements of the club.

*Subscribers list:* The subscribers list of a book club is constantly revised and not all members renew their subscription in the following year. There is a continuous upgradation of subscribers list where some members have opted out and new members have been roped in. This is generally done by providing inducements to the subscribers which may include a free book after purchase of three of four titles or price reduction in all the titles if membership is renewed in the subsequent year.

The main selection is always offered on a negative option basis, the basic principle of the book clubs all the world over. It was originally designed by Harry Scherman, founder of the 'Book of the Month Club' of America in 1926. The information about the new titles included in the book club edition is sent to the subscribers periodically (almost monthly). The subscriber has to reply back within a specified period if the subscriber does not want that title.

The negative option means that the members receive the main selection unless they notify the club that they do not want it. This is being regarded as the real secret of success of book club operation.

The system invited criticism. The book clubs in America modified it by providing more time between announcements of the new titles and dead line for declining the main selection. The negative option in one form or the other still exists in the operations of a book club. Members are also given option to select from the new list or already advertised list. This allows the club to sell their earlier published or purchased titles. New members are attracted by offering premiums for joining. Special cut rate prices are offered.

*Pricing:* As mentioned earlier the pricing of the book club edition is kept much lower than the original edition price. The clubs fix the price of the selected edition according to multiple mark up formula. Depending upon the size of the club and the number of copies it wishes to make available the club edition may be procured in one of these ways:

1. The club may opt to print its own edition.
2. The club may ask the original publisher to print desired number of copies along with the original printing.
3. The club may buy stock already published by a publisher.

The cost of publishing a book club edition normally does not include editorial cost and sometimes cost of composing and printing. In case printing is to be done by the club, the publisher would transfer films of the text, illustrations and sometimes even jackets free of charge.

In certain cases where a club decides to acquire a title after the publisher has completed its print run, it buys from publisher's own stock at what is known as 'unit cost', the cost of printing, paper, binding excluding the typesetting which is usually borne solely by the publisher.

The book club sells directly to the reader. There is no middlemen or agencies like wholesaler or distributor or retailer. Thus a clear saving in discounts which a publisher has to offer to these agencies for selling his books. This saving helps the book club to keep the selling price low.

*Wooing the Customers:* Low prices and other inducements are the main stay of book club operations. Mere fact that books can be bought cheaper through mail than in bookstores sustains the book club membership. Every book club makes an all out effort to keep the membership at a certain minimum level to make the whole operation of the book club economically viable and profitable.

For inducement of members, the clubs spend a lot of money on advertisement and promotion. Budget for both the activities is very high. Clubs make their own decision whether to spend more money on direct mail solicitation or advertisement.

It is very difficult to measure the cost effectiveness of advertisement and direct mail promotion expenditure. When a promotion method or advertisement campaign is not bringing in enough number of new members, it is the time to withdraw that campaign substituting with a new one.

For space advertisement, local media, newspapers, popular magazines and special magazines for women are used. In direct mail solicitation, the club would depend upon a specially prepared mailing list which may be drawn from selected magazines, subscription lists, membership lists of clubs and other such organisations.

Evaluation of the list on the purchasing pattern and credit worthiness of the members is done annually. Performance evaluation and cautious testing of the subscribers help the club in redefining the promotion plans.

## BOOK CLUBS AND BOOK TRADE

Some people in the industry feel that book clubs would create competition for the traditional bookshop sale. But this fear has not been substantiated by figures. Book club sales, however, have increased phenomenally. Book trade in general has never been enthusiastic about book club operations. Booksellers have always taken them as competitors sitting on a higher pedestal. The special inducements and discounted prices are deterrent for the ordinary buyer to buy from a bookshop when the book is available at much cheaper rate in a book club selection.

The only satisfaction is that a large majority of those who subscribe to book clubs are not the ones who usually buy books from bookshops. In other words the target clientele of the book clubs generally do not clash with the buyers of books from bookshops.

The brighter side is that the idea of getting books without going to the bookshop indirectly helps inculcating book reading habit. This newly initiated lovers of book reading do go to the bookshops also to buy more books to satiate their book hunger.

The advertising which book clubs do to promote titles on their selection list also attracts non club members and make them aware of the new books in the market. Should anyone of them want to buy a copy where else would one go, to the bookshop of course.

The publishing industry on the other hand has welcomed this concept. The initial hostility has disappeared. Publishers have started realising that income from book club rights sometimes outweigh the income of the book through regular sale.

Book club is a big business. It is a difficult business too. It will not let the management board to sit and relax. Even established clubs have to keep a constant watch on the kinds of books they offer, their price line, developing new tastes and adding new members. Day to day operations, new campaigns, fulfilment of orders and demands need to be carefully monitored.

The countries, where this idea of selling through mail originated, have witnessed proliferation of book clubs. Some of them may have lost in the race, others are still running to cater to a very large number of readers (who do not throng to bookshops) that still exist and perhaps continue to.

Indian publishing industry is waiting for new players to make this idea work. The market for such an experiment is very vast. What is needed is a few entrepreneurs to exploit this generally untapped potential market to the benefit of both the publishing and the public.

# Part V
# Essential Aspects of Book Publishing

# 21
# Economics of Publishing

An easy way to understand the economics of publishing is to examine the financial characteristics of publishing operation. The availability of funds, the inputs of a publishing project and factors that contribute towards income, are some of the areas which need special attention for a student of publishing economics.

Publishing industry is always starved of fund flow. It takes couple of months for the publisher to prepare the manuscript for the press and bring it out in the form of a book. After the book is published he has to wait for two to three years before the entire edition (if one is so lucky) to be sold and his investment to return. In the meantime he has to either eat up his own capital or depend upon the loans which he must have secured to sustain himself and his establishment till his out of pocket expenses are returned and profit starts.

Publishing is a difficult trade, many times more unpredictable than any other business. No publisher, however, shrewed, can tell why a book sells in thousands, while another equally promising turns out to be a total failure. It is not uncommon for the banks to make more profits on publishing activity through interest charges than the publishers make.

## FINANCE AND ITS SOURCES

For a publisher, raising finance for future planning, has always been one of the biggest problem. To enter publishing, one does not need to build a large plant or purchase expensive machinery or huge sums developing a book. But to continue doing so- publishing book after book, in a planned and purposeful manner, one needs to spend and arrange a good deal of money.

For example, in text book publishing a major new series may require an investment in lakhs of rupees. Similarly in trade book publishing intensive competition of good authors is making increasingly heavy cash demand on publishing houses.

To provide for money when it is needed most, is a crucial factor in the publisher's economics. Unless the publishing house has an unlimited cash reserve, the other way of sustaining in the industry is the fast movement of cash flow.

## CASH FLOW

The key to financial control is the flow of money through the organisation, commonly known as 'cash flow'. Cash flow is a cycle in which money is spent in order to get more money back in the form of sale of the product. Author advances, plant cost, inventory cost, all require that money be spent before books reach bookstores and sales return that money and more to the publisher.

Speed is crucial in cash flow. Faster the books get to the market and sales return the investment to the publisher, the quicker the publisher can reinvest this new money in new and better projects.

Too slow a flow creates delayed action problems. If the money does not come back fast enough to finance new programmes, the company must borrow extra money and pay additional interest cost, which in turn must be earned back in addition to the primary cost of the products. And if the borrowed money too does not return quickly enough in sales, the cycle may break down and place the firm in insolvency.

"A publisher who goes bankrupt" said Anthony Blond, "is of no use to God, Mammon or literature". A publisher, therefore, is no different from any other businessman in his pursuit of efficiency: *viz* he must watch the ratio of his overheads to his turnover. He must be concerned with cash flow; with the amount of times his stock turns over in a year.

Economics of publishing, as of any other business, works like this. A publisher begins his publishing programme with cash and attempts to increase this amount by converting it into books which can be sold out for more than what they cost. But before this cash comes back to the publisher, the original cash has to be spent on variety of purposes, which constitute the *cost* of a publisher most of which must be paid much before any sale can occur and starts the return flow which constitutes the *income*.

Thus a great deal of original amount is tied up for a long period of time. Speed of this cyclic flow—spending money by turning the amount into product and getting the money back by way of sale returns, is the key factor in the successful operation of a publishing house.

Slow returns can lead to business being closed down. It is this slow speed of cash flow which prompted experts to pronounce that 'It is easy to become a publisher, but difficult to remain one. Mortality rate at infancy is very high in this Trade'.

## REASONS FOR SLOW CASH FLOW

Publishing, like film industry, is a gamble. As a foreign expert has summed up "Out of every ten ventures, one is successful-and this is already a great deal-four make ends meet in the long run, and five make a final loss."

In order to produce a book, a publisher may have to pay thousands of rupees as advance to an author, wait for couple of months before the book is produced and a couple of more months before he can recover any money. Quite prosperous publishers have been caught between high interest rates on one hand and shortening of credit terms from paper merchants, printers and binders on the other and have run dry of cash. A publisher in this position has three option—he either sells out, merges or slows down his publishing and investment.

Before we discuss the *costs* and possible *income* of a publisher, it is worthwhile to have an idea of what are the reasons for the slow movement of cash flow in publishing industry. Slow rythme of cyclic flow in the publishing trade can be attributed to the following two major factors:

*(i)* Nature of the product
*(ii)* Nature of the consumer/customer

### *(i) Nature of the Product*

The product of book trade differs from any other manufacturer in the sense that publisher's raw material is not so much the product of automated paper mill but the complicated efforts of human mind. This factor makes the entire product a subjective thing. Each book is different. Each title a separate entity. A book has diverse functions. It acts differently on different people. Sometimes it acts differently on the same person in different situations.

It is, therefore, difficult to anticipate the demand for a book. Publishers are, therefore, confronted with the problem of under production and over production. Another peculiarity of this trade is the value of the unsold stock. Unsold copies deem to have negative value for the publisher since they add to his overheads without yielding any income.

The sale or profit on books is guided by the principle of demand. A book is not worth the paper it is printed on unless it is demanded by someone. The value of unsold books is less than that of old newspapers, the cost of binding in such cases is a total loss.

### *(ii) Nature of the Customer/Consumer*

As the nature of the product is peculiar so is the nature of the customer/consumer. As mentioned earlier each book is different, it does not have a universal appeal unless the thought contents of a book are identified with the specific needs of the reader, he may not look at it.

There are two types of buyers. (1) Individuals and (2) Institutions. Individual buyers are fast diminishing because of financial constraints and increase in the cost of books. In most other consumer products individual buyers are the main stay of the economy. Individual buyers serve as the quick cash transactors and responsible for fast return of the sale proceeds to the manufacturer.

In book publishing the situation is just the opposite. Bulk of the quantity published goes to the institutions. Institutions are slow pay masters. They enjoy the privilege of making payments at ease. Some institutions look towards their parent bodies for release of grants. Institutions are not located at one place. They are scattered allover the country and therefore takes a long time for the money to return.

All these factors make publishing a highly under capitalised business. An institution does not pay back in time to the bookseller, the bookseller delays the payment to the wholesaler and the wholesaler in turn is helpless to pay the publisher in time. The publisher, thus delays the payment to the printer, paper merchant etc. In such a situation a publisher has to strike a good balance between his costs and possible income.

A publisher, no matter big or small, has to keep a keen eye on the investment cost, break even point, income and possible profits to keep the entire operation of book publishing economical. In order to understand in detail these factors are discussed below individually.

## COST

A publisher's cost is a complex term. It includes categories of costs that will have to be taken into account while determining the publishing cost of a book. It is against this cost that publisher will think making any profit.

There are many ways to understand the cost of a publishing project. The following methods would give a clear picture of categories of cost that constitute the cost of publishing a book.

1. Printing Factor Method
2. Operation Factor Method
3. Cost Factor Method

All these methods are to arrive at the same conclusion-to determine the publishing cost.

1. *Printing Factor Method:* In this method the whole process of publishing is divided into two sectors *i.e.* (i) pre-printing costs, and (ii) printing costs.

Pre-printing costs would include editorial preparation cost, cost of finding the author and payment of advances, book designing, securing estimates and appointment of printer. It would also include various overheads of the publishing house. The cost of typesetting, plate making and all other costs upto the point of sending the matter to the press are covered under this segment.

Printing costs would include production work, cost of press work, cost of binding, cost of promotion, selling, storage and other general overheads on these items. It may also include interest cost on capital which the publisher may have borrowed in the process.

2. *Operation Factor Method:* This is another way of looking at the publisher's *costs.* In this method the whole process of publishing is divided into various operations and the costs incurred on them is

calculated. The various operations in the process of book publishing can be enumerated as follows:

(i) Editorial preparation
(ii) Physical manufacture and production
(iii) Sales promotion and marketing costs
(iv) Administrative overheads

*(i) Editorial Preparation:* These costs would include the amount spent by the publishing house on the preparation of manuscript for the press. It includes procuring the manuscript from the author, fees paid to outside expert for evaluating the manuscript, payment of advances, editing and copy editing, designing and payments to artists etc.

*(ii) Physical Manufacture and Production Costs:* It includes costs incurred by the publisher on composing; typesetting, printing, proof reading, paper and binding. It would also include payments made to any other agency or individual involved in the physical manufacture of the book.

*(iii) Sales Promotion and Marketing Costs:* These are the expenses incurred by the publisher on promotion and publicity of the book. The expenditure made on printing of publicity material, salaries of the staff in the sales department and other incidental costs involved in the promotion and sale of the book. Marketing expenses such as cost of catalogues, circulars, direct mail, posters, displays and other such exhibits is also grouped under this head.

*(iv) Administrative Overheads:* All such costs which cannot be directly attributed to the above heads are covered under the overheads. These costs include, rent, salaries to administrative staff, taxes, payment of telephone bills, telegraph and other postal charges, costs of light and power and maintenance of the premises etc.

3. *Cost Factor Method:* The cost in publishing is a subjective expression. It is linked with the size of the edition. It varies if the number of copies to be printed is increased or decreased. Publishing cost is guided by the principle that manufacturing cost per copy goes down not just a little but often substantially as the quantity increases. It is not only true in manufacturing cost but also other operating expenses of a publisher.

The principle though easy to pronounce, yet difficult to practice because you have to spend money to earn money. It is common knowledge that larger the edition, smaller the cost of production. But whether this advantage can be availed of by the publisher, is a difficult question to answer.

If a publisher publishes a bigger edition in order to reduce cost and is unable to sell the edition, he looses more money in the process. On the other hand if he decides to print a smaller edition, he will have to increase the selling price to neutralise the higher cost of production. Thus jeopardising the chances of higher sale because of high selling price.

Publisher's cost, therefore, has to be studied from the point of view of cost related to the size of the edition. These can be divided as follows:

*(i)* Costs related to the length of the book.

*(ii)* Costs related to the number of copies printed.

*(iii)* General and administrative costs which are more or less fixed but not related to costs in (i) and (ii).

*(iv)* Out of pocket advertising costs.

This is not a very methodical division of costs. Because large part of the editorial expenses except for copy editing is not related to the length of the book or number of pages. Similarly the expenses on illustrations and design work is not largely related to the size of the edition. But if the expenses are to be allocated to individual books for the purpose of estimating total costs, this kind of cost analysis can be useful.

More simpler and accurate method of calculating cost is to divide the total operational costs into fixed and variable costs. Promotion and overhead costs are added to arrive at the publishing cost of a book. Since this method is related to the size of the edition, it is easier to understand how these heads of costs are influenced by the number of copies to be printed.

These costs can be conveniently subdivided as follows:

### 1. *Fixed Costs or Unvarying Costs*

Fixed costs have been defined as costs which tend to be unaffected by variations in volume of output. These costs arise due to contractual obligations of management decisions. The examples of fixed costs are rent, salaries, taxes etc. which a publisher has to pay irrespective of the number of titles produced and number of copies printed. Under certain circumstances these costs also change but the change is not related to one single factor. These costs do not vary or change no matter whether 1000 copies or 500 copies are printed.

Costs involved in editorial preparation of manuscript, copy editing, payment made to outside expert etc. are examples of fixed costs which have no bearing on the size of the edition.

At production stage, the composing charges, typesetting, plate making, payment to artist for making illustrations and such other charges before the printer turns the press for actual printing are covered under fixed or unvarying costs as these costs remain the same irrespective of the number of copies to be printed.

Promotion costs such as discount to wholesalers and retailers, salaries to despatch and sales staff are more or less fixed costs depending upon the policy of a publishing house. Many publishers plan to spend a fixed percentage of the year's sale income on advertising. Therefore, such costs are considered fixed costs.

Overhead costs more or less are also fixed costs. All costs can not be attributed directly to the output of goods and services. Expenses such as rent, taxes, interest on capital and other expenses of administration and accounts are covered under overheads. In other words, overheads include the cost of the staff by department and their expenditure, publicity and promotional costs which are required to meet the objective of the publishing house.

2. *Unfixed or Varying Costs*

Variable costs are those costs which vary directly or proportionately with the output. These costs are linked with the size of the edition printed and expected to be sold. These costs would automatically vary if the number of copies to be printed is increased or reduced.

*(i)* Unless the author has been promised a lump sum money as copyright fee for the book, the payment of royalty depends upon the number of copies sold by the publisher.

*(ii)* The cost of printing a book, the cost of paper as well as binding expenses are good examples of varying costs. A 3000 copy edition would need three times the paper needed for a 1000 copy edition. Similarly, the cost of binding of 3000 copies would also be proportionately higher than binding charges for 1000 copies. These costs remain fluctuating with the number of copies printed.

*(iii)* Promotion and other marketing expenses are also linked with the size of the edition. Promotion and advertising budget is usually decided keeping in mind the number of copies to be printed. Some publishers, though, fix their promotion budget, but for each individual title, how much is to be spent, is generally guided by the number of copies expected to be sold.

*(iv)* The term overhead may be defined as the aggregate of indirect material cost, indirect wages and indirect expenses. The expenses that cannot be allocated to a single direct expense head are known as overheads. These overheads, generally fixed, are also influenced to some extent with the increase in volume of turnover.

The overhead expenses pertaining to a title produced are charged and added to the cost of production. For this purpose overhead rates of expenses for adding them to production cost may be estimated on the following basis:

*(i)* The figure of the previous year or period may be adopted as the overhead rate to be charged on production in the current year.

*(ii)* The overhead rate for the titles may be determined on the basis of estimated expenses and estimated volume of production activity.

*(iii)* Overhead cost is calculated on the basis of percentage of net sales income as it was in the previous year.

Accordingly, if the net sales income totalled Rs. 5,00,000 and overhead cost totalled Rs. 1,00,000, it will be assumed that the overhead in the coming year would be 20 percent of net sales income.

Whatever method is applied to work out the cost of overhead expenses, the fact remains that certain percentage of such expenses is added to the unit cost of production to determine the unit cost as well as the unit sale price.

Costs, therefore, play a very significant role in publishing management. One way to reduce cost is to print larger editions. But if a publisher cannot sell 1000 copies, why should he publish 5000 copies just to reduce the cost of production.

From the above discussion, it is amply clear that production cost consists of fixed as well as unfixed costs. Though unfixed costs vary with the size of the edition, fixed costs or unvariable costs remain the same and thereby reduce the unit cost of production considerably with the increase in the size of the edition.

The following chart would illustrate how increase in number of copies reduces the unit cost of production. Let us take an example of book of 160 pages in demy octavo size with hard bound section sewn with double colour cover design. The rates used in the example are only imaginary and may not be related to the prevailing market rates. It is clear from the above example that though the cost of production increases from Rs.18050 for 1000 copies to Rs. 44450 for 3000 copies, the unit cost of production decreases from Rs.18.05 for 1000 copy edition to Rs. 14.81 for 3000 copy edition.

Table 1

Production Cost

| | 1000 Copies Rs. | 3000 Copies Rs. | 5000 Copies Rs. |
|---|---|---|---|
| *Fixed Costs* | | | |
| Editorial charges | 750 | 750 | 750 |
| Composing and Typesetting charges @ Rs. 20 per page | 3200 | 3200 | 3200 |
| Cover design | 400 | 400 | 400 |
| Cover block | 500 | 500 | 500 |
| | 4850 | 4850 | 4850 |
| *Unfixed or Variable Costs* | | | |
| Text printing @ Rs. 10 per page per thousand | 1600 | 4800 | 8000 |
| Cover printing @ Rs. 100 per colour per thousand | 200 | 600 | 1000 |
| Binding charges @ Rs. 5 per copy | 5000 | 15000 | 25000 |
| Paper for text @ Rs. 300 per ream | 6000 | 18000 | 30000 |
| Paper for cover Rs. 600 per ream | 400 | 1200 | 2000 |
| | 13200 | 39600 | 66000 |
| Fixed Cost | 4850 | 4850 | 4850 |
| Unfixed cost | 13200 | 39600 | 66000 |
| Total | 18050 | 44450 | 70850 |
| | Rs. P. | Rs. P. | Rs. P. |
| Unit cost (approx.) | 18.05 | 14.81 | 14.17 |

It is also to be noted that difference in the unit cost of production between 3000 copy edition and 5000 copy edition is only paise 64 but there is lot of difference in cost of production. Therefore, in such a situation it is economical to print 3000 copy edition or 1000 copy edition.

## INCOME

Publisher's income is dependent upon the books he sells and not the books he publishes. There is no wisdom in enlarging the size of the edition just to decrease the cost of production if a publisher can not sell that number or enough of it to register any profit. On the other hand, if he miscalculates the sale potential of the book and publishes smaller edition than the actual market demand, he looses both time and money.

The guiding principles of economics of publishing are: (i) Reducing cost by Rs. 1000 would have similar effect on the profit and loss statement as increasing sale by several thousands, and (ii) you have to spend money to make money.

It is here the business acumen of a publisher plays a vital role. Income from a publishing project depends upon the following factors:

1. *Selling Price:* Selling price of a book is fixed after determining the unit cost of production. Selling price has a direct bearing on the profit and loss of a publisher. If selling price is high, the break even, where cost of production is recovered, would be low and if larger number of copies are sold, a publisher can hope to harvest a rich profit. Selling price is fixed by multiplying the cost of production a number of times, usually four to six times, depending upon the nature of the book and nature of the clientele. This fixing of selling price by multiplying the manufacturing cost to cover the additional costs and profit is called mark up. The mark up would differ from book to book and publisher to publisher.

For purpose of understanding, let us presume that in the case of cost worked out in Table 1 the mark up is fixed at 3 times the manufacturing cost. The selling price, therefore, in this case would be as shown in Table 2.

Table 2
Selling Price

| | 1000 Copies<br>Rs. P. | 3000 Copies<br>Rs. P. | 5000 Copies<br>Rs. P. |
|---|---|---|---|
| Unit cost | 18.05 | 14.81 | 14.17 |
| Selling price<br>with 3 times mark up | 54.15 | 44.43 | 42.51 |

After deducting various costs, it would reveal whether selling price with 3 times mark up is economically viable or not.

2. *Number of Copies Sold:* How many copies would be sold has always been the cause of anxiety among the publishers. No publisher, however, shrewed, can tell why a book sells in thousands, while another equally promising turns out to be a total failure. Publishers, therefore, are prone to taking risks.

If the prediction comes true, a publisher makes profit. The watch word is how many copies can be sold and how soon. This is a very crucial factor in determining a publisher's income. The number of copies sold over and above the break even point would add to publisher's profit. A percentage of' the edition is distributed free as specimen copies and review copies.

3. *Trade and Other Discounts:* Trade discount is reduction from the stated or list price which booksellers demand and publishers offer, to sell the books. Apart from usual trade discount, some times additional and extra discounts are also offered depending upon factors like special occasions, cash payment, quantity purchase, pre-publication offer etc. The ultimate buyer may sometimes pay the list price but a publisher always gets back money after deducting the percentage or amount of discount on the selling price. The discounts vary from 30% to 50% depending upon the nature of the book and other related factors. Slow selling titles attract more discount than text books which sell faster and also in multiple.

The net sales income received back by a publisher after deducting trade discount, therefore, is much less than the printed price of the book. Table below will illustrate the point.

Table 3
Selling Price and Net Sales Income

| | 1000 Copies<br>Rs. P. | 3000 Copies<br>Rs. P. | 5000 Copies<br>Rs. P. |
|---|---|---|---|
| Unit Cost | 18.05 | 14.81 | 14.17 |
| Selling price three times the cost of production | 54.15 | 44.43 | 42.51 |
| Less discount @ 33-1/3 percent | 18.05 | 14.81 | 14.17 |
| Net sales income after deducting trade discount | 36.10 | 29.62 | 28.34 |
| Copies available for sale | 900 copies | 2800 copies | 4800 copies |
| Total Net Sales Income if all copies are sold | 32490.00 | 82936.00 | 136032.00 |

4. *Marketing and Other Incidental Costs:* These are incidental expenses on marketing and promotion of books. It also includes direct overheads. There is no fixed set of rules to calculate the marketing expenses. The percentage of such expenses varies from publisher to publisher. To be on safer side, most publishers earmark 10% of the net sales income as marketing and other incidental expenses. There are others who calculate these costs from 5 to 7 per cent of the physical manufacture cost.

Incidental costs also include rentals, interest on capital and borrowings etc. Overheads are usually calculated on the net sales income and should ideally remain .on the lower side. Ten to twelve percent of net sales income is considered adequate overhead expenses.

On the basis of the above mentioned costs the total publishing cost of a title is worked out. The total publishing cost of the example taken in previous tables would be as follows:

Table 4
Total Publishing Cost

| | 1000 Copies<br>Rs. P. | 3000 Copies<br>Rs. P. | 5000 Copies<br>Rs. P. |
|---|---|---|---|
| Production cost<br>(From Table 1) | 18050.00 | 44450.00 | 70850.00 |
| Author's royalty @ 10% of selling price | 4873.00 | 12440.00 | 20404.00 |
| Promotion and Publicity cost @ 10%<br>of production cost | 1805.00 | 4445.00 | 7085.00 |
| Administrative overheads @ 10% of Net<br>Sales Income (From Table 3) | 3249.00 | 8293.00 | 13603.00 |
| Total publishing cost<br>(figures have been rounded off to nearest rupee) | 27977.00 | 69628.00 | 111942.00 |

## WHAT IS THE PROFIT

The difference between the sales income and total publishing cost is the possible profit of a publisher. This exercise of possible profit is necessary to arrive at a decision regarding the size of the edition as well as the selling price of the publication.

The possible profit in this case if all the copies are sold is shown in the following table:

Table 5
Possible Profit if all Copies are Sold

| | 1000 Copies Rs. P. | 3000 Copies Rs. P. | 5000 Copies Rs. P. |
|---|---|---|---|
| Total sales income | 32490.00 | 82936.00 | 136032.00 |
| Total publishing cost | 27977.00 | 69628.00 | 111942.00 |
| Possible profit | 4513.00 | 13308.00 | 24090.00 |
| Percentage of profit on publishing cost | 16.13 | 19.11 | 21.52 |

If a publisher considers that the possible percentage of profit against investment is low and that it does not cover the usual interest on capital investment, the mark up may be increased by 4 or 5 times.

In this case explained in the tables above if the selling price is fixed at 4 times the unit cost of production the margin of profit will shoot up.

The percentage of profit in this case would become more than 41% in case of 1000 copy edition; 44% in case of 3000 copy edition and 47% in case of 5000 copy edition.

From such calculations a publisher is able to determine in advance the economic edition that would bring reasonable profit for the investment made. In this case the margin of profit for 1000 copy edition with 4 times mark up appears to be more economical because the difference in percentage between 1000 copy edition and 3000 copy edition is only marginal but there is huge difference between the total publishing cost between the two editions.

Table 6
Percentage of Possible Profit with 4 Times Mark Up

| | 1000 Copies Rs. P. | 3000 Copies Rs. P. | 5000 Copies Rs. P. |
|---|---|---|---|
| Unit cost of production | 18.05 | 14.81 | 14.17 |
| Selling price 4 times the unit cost of production | 72.20 | 59.24 | 56.68 |
| Less trade discount @ 33-1/3% of selling price | 24.06 | 19.74 | 18.89 |
| Net sales income per copy | 48.14 | 39.50 | 37.79 |
| Number of copies expected to be sold | 900 copies | 2800 copies | 4800 copies |
| Net sales income for the edition | 43326.00 | 110600.00 | 181392.00 |
| Total publishing cost | 18050.00 | 44450.00 | 70850.00 |
| Author's royalty @ 10% of production cost | 1805.00 | 4445.00 | 7085.00 |
| Administrative overheads @ 10% of net sales income | 4332.00 | 11060.00 | 18139.00 |
| | 30685.00 | 76542.00 | 12380.00 |
| Possible profit if all copies are sold | 43326.00 | 110600.00 | 181392.00 |
| (Net sales income - Total publishing cost) | – 30685.00 | – 76542.00 | – 123280.00 |
| | 12641.00 | 34058.00 | 58112.00 |
| Profit percentage of total publishing cost | 41% (41.19) | 44% (44.49) | 47% (47.13) |

Pricing formula affects the profit margin of a publisher which may vary with each book. Different criteria is applied for fixing the price of each book produced. Break even point is calculated before finalizing the selling price of a book.

## BREAK EVEN POINT

Calculations of possible profit margin are made on the presumption that all the copies of an edition would be sold. In actual practice this happens only but rarely. A publisher, therefore, has to assure while fixing the selling price that even if the entire edition is not sold, how many copies he would have to sell so that his out of pocket expenses are recovered.

Publishers, therefore, try to calculate the 'break even point' for each title in order to know the number of copies that must be sold before the book starts bringing in any profit. This is also known as 'get out point' as after reaching this point or stage the publisher has recovered the cost of production and therefore gets out of the danger of loosing money on the book.

Break even point may be defined as the 'estimated point or stage at which net receipts equal net costs outlay on a book'. It is the intersection of costs and prices in a break even analysis. A no profit no loss stage in publishing when a publisher has sold a specific number of copies to equal his investment. It is an analysis of expenses aimed at determining at what cost and price points, a product, a book or a company breaks even.

At this point or level the sales revenues are just equal to the costs incurred. Below this level the publishing house will make losses, while above this level, it will be making profits.

This exercise is done before the selling price has been finalised. If at this stage it is felt that the break even point is on the higher side, alternate break even point is arrived at by making possible changes in the costs as well the selling price of the product.

Publishers often calculate the margin per copy after deducting the expenses to meet the cost of production. The total cost of production is then divided by the margin per copy. The resultant figure would give a rough idea as to how many copies need to be sold in order to recover the cost of production or reach the break even.

## HOW TO CALCULATE BREAK EVEN POINT

Break even point is a helpful tool in assessing the performance of a publishing house with regards to a particular book. For calculating break even point certain inputs are necessary. These are:

Expected selling price
Trade discount
Fixed costs
Unfixed costs
Percentage of author's royalty
Percentage of overheads (both administrative and promotional)
Size of the edition etc.

Break even point is calculated as follows:

Step 1. Selling price (SP) less Trade Discount (TD) = Net sales income (NSI)

Step 2. Net sales income (NSI) less Author's Royalty (AR) and overheads (OH) = Sales income (SI)

Step 3. Cost of production (CP) divided by sales Income (SI) = Break Even Point (BEP)

This can be represented as follows:

SP – TD = NSI
NSI – AR + OH = SI
CP ÷ SI = BEP

The break even point for 1000 copy edition of a book whose costs have been worked out in the tables above with selling price three times the unit cost of production would be as follows:

| | Rs. P. | |
|---|---|---|
| Selling price | 54.15 | |
| Trade Discount @ 33-1/3% | 18.05 | |
| | 36.10 | Net sales income |
| Net sales income | 36.10 | |
| Less Author's Royalty | | |
| @ 10% of selling price | 5.41 | |
| | 30.69 | |
| Less overheads per copy | 7.22 | |
| @ 20% of Net sales income | 23.47 | Sales income per copy |

Cost of production ÷ (From (table 1) Sales income per copy $= \frac{18050}{23.47} = 769$ copies

Break Even Point = 769 copies

It is to be noticed that the break even at 769 copies is on the higher side. This is so because selling price is estimated at three times the unit cost of production in a 1000 copy edition.

Break even point for the same book with selling price estimated at four times the unit cost of production would bring down the break even point considerably.

| | Rs. P. |
|---|---|
| Selling price | 72.20 |
| Trade Discount @ 33-1/3% | 24.06 |
| Net sales income | 48.14 |
| Net sales income | 48.14 |
| Less Author's Royalty @ 10% of selling price | 7.22 |
| | 40.92 |
| Less overheads @ 20% of Net Sales Income | 9.62 |
| Margin per copy/Sales income Cost of production | 31.30 |

(From Table 1) ÷ Sales Income per copy $\frac{18050}{31.30} = 576$

Break even point = 576 copies

This is nearly 200 copies less than the first proposition.

In terms of percentage the break even point arrives at 57.6 percent of the 1000 copy edition as against 76.9 percent if the selling price is fixed at four times the unit cost of production instead of three times.

*Advantages*

1. It is possible to know the probable profitability of a product besides the level of no profit no loss. Publishers can boost its promotional and marketing activities to reach the break even level as quickly as possible.

2. The exercise provides an opportunity to give a second thought and reorganise variable costs at different levels of book production.
3. It gives an idea of fixed costs in book production. Publishers can take remedial measures to control such costs.
4. Break even analysis is helpful in forecasting, long term planning and growth of the publishing house.

*Limitations*

Break even analysis has no doubt become an important tool to assess and forecast the financial commitment in a publishing project, it has certain limitations.

1. Fixed costs do not always remain constant. For example, overheads, which are more or less considered fixed costs, do vary from time to time.
2. Marginal and unfixed costs do not vary proportionately.
3. Since each book will have its own break even analysis, break even analysis for the publishing house as a whole becomes undependable.
4. The costs incurred on growth and expansion of the business sometimes, do not get reflected in the break even analysis for each individual book brought out by a publishing house.

## PROFIT PLANNING IN A PUBLISHING HOUSE

The primary success factor in any business is the capability of the management to plan and control its activities to accomplish the specific objectives of the enterprise. Publishing management, therefore, would include, besides publishing books, planning of activities and their control to achieve success as a financial venture.

It is an accepted fact that profit level in publishing is much lower. It is generally said that if you can make money in publishing, you can make much more money in any other business.

It is a difficult occupation. Profit margins vary with pricing formula adopted for each title and category of books. Planning future projects, raising capital has always been one of major problems for the publishing fraternity.

Do not forget that publishing has rewards to offer far greater than money. For real publishing extends beyond monetary or mercantile interests. For those interested only in cash dividends, the cultural and intangible profits of great publishing are meaningless.

# 22

# International Standard Book Number

## ISBN DEFINED

ISBN or sometimes pronounced 'Is-ben' is an acronym for International Standard Book Number. It is given to every book or edition of a book before publication to identify the publisher, the edition and volume number.

## WHAT IS AN ISBN?

The ISBN (International Standard Book Number) is a unique machine-readable identification number, which marks any book unmistakably. This number is defined in ISO Standard 2108. The number has been in use now for 30 years and has revolutionized the international book-trade. 166 countries and territories are officially ISBN members. The ISBN accompanies a publication from its production onwards.

## BACKGROUND

W.H. Smith, the booksellers and stationers developed the ISBN system in United Kingdom in 1966 and was originally called Standard Book Number or SB. International Organization recommended the system for international use for Standards (ISO) in October 1969. It was accepted by the delegates of the Plenary Session and circulated to all member bodies in 1970.

The ten-digit number with last digit as check digit is said to have only 2 to 3 percent of error rate in ISBN.

## PURPOSE

The purpose of this international standard is to coordinate and standardize the international use of ISBNs to uniquely identify one title or edition of a title, published by one specific publisher.

The main functions of the International ISBN Agency are:

- To promote, coordinate and supervise the world-wide use of the ISBN system.
- To approve the definition and structure of group agencies.
- To allocate group identifiers to group agencies.
- To advise on the establishment and functioning of group agencies.
- To advise group agencies on the allocation of international publisher identifiers.
- To publish the assigned group numbers and publishers' prefixes in up-to-date form.

## STRUCTURE OF ISBN

The ISBN is divided into four parts of variable length, which must be separated clearly by hyphens or spaces:

ISBN 81-241-0614-2 *or* ISBN 81 241 0614 2

These parts are as follows:

- Group identifier
- Publisher identifier
- Title identifier
- Check digit

## GROUP IDETIFIER NUMBER

First group of digits are group identifier and indicate a national, geographical, language or other convenient group. The group may be of single digit or multiple digits. The country field is 0 or 1 for English speaking countries, 2 for French speaking countries, and 3 for German speaking countries. The country field can be 5 digits long. For example 99936 are used for Bhutan. The country code for India is 81 and 93. The complete list of countries, which have been allotted group code, is available with the International Book Number Agency in Berlin, Germany.

## PUBLISHER IDETIFIER NUMBER

The publisher identifier number, which may also consist of multiple digits, is awarded by the National Standard Book Number Agency in each country. In India, Raja Ram Mohan Roy Library Foundation established by the government of India has been entrusted with the job of assigning the publisher code and also the block code to the publishers according to their requirements.

## NUMBERS FOR INDIVIDUAL TITLES

The National Standard Book Number Agency gives the numbers in block of ten to hundred some times even more at a time according to the publishing program of a publisher. After the block of numbers received by the publisher is utilized the Agency is intimated and further block may be asked for. In this way a small publisher may receive an ISBN consisting if one digit for the language, seven digits for the publisher and single digit for the individual item. Once that block is used up, the publisher can receive another block of numbers. As a consequence different publisher number may correspond to the same publisher.

The individual item/title number follows the publisher code.

## THE CHECK DIGIT

The check digit is the last digit of an ISBN. It is calculated on a modulus 11 with weights 10-2, using X in lieu of 10 where ten would occur as a check digit. This means that each of the first nine digits of the ISBN excluding the check digit itself is multiplied by a number ranging from 10 to 2 and that the resulting sum of the products, plus the check digit, must be divisible by 11 without a remainder.

For example: ISBN 81-241-0614-2

This is the final digit of the 10 digit ISBN. This is given to check any mistake in granting the ISBN. The check digit is a form of redundancy check used for error detection. The final character of an ISBN is a check digit computed so that multiplying each digit by its position in the number (counting from right) and taking the sum of their product modulo 11, is 0.That is the sum total of the digits multiplied by its position from the right is divisible by eleven with no remainder left. The last digit, which is multiplied by 1, is the check digit chosen to make the sum correct and divisible by 11. If the sum total of the first nine digits thus arrived is divisible by 11 then the check digit is expressed as 0.

## PARTS OF THE ISBN

ISBN consists of 10 digits (Arabic 0-9). These digits are formally broken into four parts and these parts appear on the book with the use of hyphen or space in between the parts.

For example: 81-241-0614-2 or 81 241 0614 2

| | |
|---|---|
| 1. *Part* one is group/country/language identifier | 81 (INDIA) |
| 2. *Part* two is publisher identifier | 241 (PUBLISHER CODE) |
| 3. *Par*t three is the number assigned to each individual title | 0614 (ITEM/TITLE CODE) |
| 4. *Part* four is the check number or checksum character | 2 (CHECK DIGIT) |

The number of digits in the first three parts of the ISBN (group identifier, publisher prefix, title identifier) varies. The number of digits in the group number and in the publisher prefix is determined by the quantity of titles planned to be produced by the publisher or publisher group. Publishers or publisher groups with large title outputs are represented by fewer digits.

## ADMINISTRATION OF ISBN

The administration of the ISBN system is carried out on three levels:
1. International agency 2. Group agencies 3. Publisher level

## INTERNATIONAL ADMINISTRATION

The international administration and co-ordination of the ISBN system is done through the:

International Standard Book Number Agency with HQ in Berlin, GERMANY. The main functions of the International ISBN Agency are:

To promote, coordinate and supervise the world-wide use of the ISBN system.

To allocate group identifiers to group agencies.

To publish the assigned group numbers and publishers' prefixes in up-to-date form.

## INDIA

The International Standard Book Number (ISBN) system was put into operation in January 1985 as Raja Rammohun Roy National Agency for ISBN, India, by the Ministry of Human Resource Development, Department of Secondary and Higher Education, New Delhi.

*Contact address*

Raja Rammohun Roy
National Agency for ISBN
Government of India
Ministry of Human Resource Development
Department of Secondary & Higher Education
A2/W 4, Curzon Road Barracks
New Delhi 110001
E-mail: isbn@nic.in

*Check digit in 10 digit ISBN*

Let us take the example of an ISBN 81-241-0614-2

8 x 10 = 80
1 x 9 = 9
2 x 8 = 16
4 x 7 = 28
1 x 6 = 6
0 x 5 = 0
6 x 4 = 24
1 x 3 = 3
4 x 2 = 8

Total 174

If we divide this figure with 11 the remainder will be 9. We need to add 2 to make it divisible by 11. If we add this number (2) to 174, it will make 176, which is equally divided by 11. Therefore, the check digit is 2, which is the last digit of the above ISBN. The number, therefore, is correct.

*Conversion to ISBN-13*

Rapid world wide expansion of barcode scanning has brought into prominence the agreement reached between European Access number

(EAN) and Universal Code Council (UCC) which allowed 10 digit ISBN to be converted into 13 digits. This has made ISBN an internationally identifier with world wide bar code system.

The agreement replaced the 10 digit ISBN with a special 'bookland' identifier represented by the digit '978' for books. Digit. 978 is prefixed by first nine digits of an ISBN and check digit is worked out on the basis of EAN rules (Modulus 10). The 13 digit new ISBN format increased the available numbers of ISBNs world wide and enabled conformity to the EAN global numbering system.

Beginning from January 1, 2007, ISBN agencies all over the world were asked to assign new ISBN numbers that are 13 digits long, replacing the 10 digit numbers that were currently provided.

Since it was not possible to convert systems and data to from 10 digits 13 digits ISBN overnight, the book industry promoted a dual numbering system to be used from January 1, 2005. It suggested completion by January 1, 2006 and change over to complete before 1 January 2007. Dual numbering means that a publisher may give both a book's ISBN-10 and ISBN-13 on the books. The purpose of the dual numbering approach was to allow each organization to make the transition at its own pace, instead of subjecting the industry to an abrupt manner. Transition to the ISBN-13 was to be completed as soon as possible and after January 1, 2007 ISBN-13 became officially the "ISBN" and the ISBN-10 was phased out.

## CHECK DIGIT IN ISBN 13

The International ISBN Agency's official 2005 manual covering ISBNs issued beginning January 2007, reveals the 13-digit ISBN *check digit*, which is the last digit of the 13-digit ISBN, is calculated differently from the old 10-digit ISBN *check digit*. The ISBN 13 *check digit* is calculated on a *modulus* 10 of the alternately weighted (by 1 and 3) products of the first 12 digits, with additional calculation of this result.

Calculating an ISBN 13 *check digit* requires that each of the first twelve digits of the 13-digit ISBN—excluding the *check digit* itself—be multiplied alternately by 1 and 3. Next, take the sum *modulo* 10 of these products. This result is subtracted from 10. The result is the check digit. If the check digit calculates to 10, 0 is used.

Let us take the example of ISBN ISBN 81-241-0614-2
Pre fix 978 to the 10 digit ISBN ISBN 978-81- 241- 0614-

9 x 1 = 9
7 x 3 = 2 1
8 x 1 = 8
8 x 3 = 2 4
1 x 1 = 1
2 x 3 = 6
4 x 1 = 4
1 x 3 = 3
0 x 1 = 0
6 x 3 = 1 8
1 x 1 = 1
4 x 3 = 1 2

Total 107

When we divide 107 by 10 the remainder is 7. The result is subtracted from 10. The resultant 3 is the check digit in 13 number ISBN.

The complete sequence of 13 digit ISBN is 978-81-241-0614 - 3

## PRINTING OF ISBN

The ISBN must appear on the item itself. This is essential for the efficient running of the system.

The ISBN must appear:

- on the verso of the title page (copyright page);
- on the lower section of the outside back cover;
- on the foot of the title page, if there is no space elsewhere;
- on the bottom of the back dust jacket, or any other protective case, or wrapper; and
- on the base of the spine (only if the product is a paperback book).

*Advantages of the ISBN*

- The ISBN is a unique international identifier for monographic publications; the ten-digit number (now 13 digits) therefore replaces the handling of long bibliographic descriptive records. Time and staff are saved, copying mistakes are avoided.

- The ISBN allows compilation and updating of book-trade directories, like Books in Print. Information on available books can be easily found.
- Ordering and distribution of books is mainly executed by ISBN; this is a fast and efficient method.
- The ISBN is machine-readable in the form of a 13-digit Bookland EAN bar code. This is fast and avoids mistakes.
- The ISBN is needed for the running of electronic point-of-sale systems in bookshops.
- Rights management is mainly done on the basis of ISBN.
- Sales data monitoring is done by ISBN.
- Libraries profit from copy-cataloguing by ISBN.
- The national lending right in some countries is based on ISBN.

## CARE IN USING ISBN

*Publishers with more than one place of publication*

a. A publisher operating in several places which are listed together in the imprint of the book will assign only one ISBN to the book.
b. A publisher operating separate and distinct offices or branches in different places may have a publisher identifier for each office or branch. However, each book published is to be assigned only one ISBN. This ISBN should be assigned by the office or branch responsible for publication.

## REGISTRATION OF ISBN

It is the responsibility of all publishers to inform their group agency or the organization responsible for the maintenance of title registration of the ISBNs that have been assigned to published and forthcoming books. When the publisher does not take this responsibility, the group agency or the organization responsible for the maintenance of title registration is authorized to maintain the ISBN register of this publisher on its own initiative.

## ISBN CAN NEVER BE RE-USED

An ISBN, once assigned, can never be re-used, under any circumstances. This is of the utmost importance to avoid confusion.

If, through a clerical error, a number is incorrectly assigned, the number must be deleted from the list of useable numbers and must never be assigned to another title.

Publishers should advise the group agency of the number(s) deleted and of the titles to which they were erroneously assigned.

It may be added here that there is, in general, no requirement for a publisher to assign an ISBN to a book or for that to display its number, but in the age of computers and Internet selling many booksellers may find it more convenient to deal in books that carry an ISBN.

# 23

# Understanding Intellectual Property—Indian Copyright Law and Problem of Piracy

## INTELLECTUAL PROPERTY DEFINED

Intellectual Property refers to creations by individuals. These may be musical. literary, artistic work or may be symbols, names and designes that can be used for the economic benefit of the creator. This includes copyrights, trademarks, patents and other related rights. Like immovable property, intellectual property also bestows certain rights to the creator. The term "intellectual property" denotes the specific legal rights, and not the intellectual work itself

Intellectual property rights are used on goods which are enjoyed by many people simultaneously—the use by one person does not exclude use by another. This is called use on non rival goods. For example, any number of people may make use of a book simultaneously or play a cassette. Since copies can these days be prepared at marginal cost. Therefore, there is a need for protection of such property. The laws provide legal protection to the owners of intellectual property. Such laws are known as Intellectual Property laws.

Intellectual property rights give creators exclusive rights to their creations, thereby providing an incentive for the author or inventor to develop and share the information rather than keep it secret. The legal protections granted by IP laws are credited with significant contributions toward economic growth.

## HUMAN RIGHTS DECLARATION ARTICLE 27(1948)

1. Everyone has the right freely to participate in the cultural life of the community, to enjoy the arts and to share in scientific advancement and its benefits.

2. Everyone has the right freely to the protection of the moral and material interests resulting from any scientific, literary or artistic production of which he is the author.

## WHAT IS COPYRIGHT?

Copyright is a right given by the law to creators of literary, dramatic, musical and artistic works and producers of cinematograph films and sound recordings. In fact, it is a bundle of rights including, *inter alia,* rights of reproduction, communication to the public, adaptation and translation of the work.

## IS THERE A NEED FOR COPYRIGHT?

Copyright provides protection of the rights of authors over their creations, thereby safeguarding and rewarding creativity. Creativity being the keystone of progress, no civilized society can afford to ignore the basic requirement of encouraging the same. Economic and social development of a society is dependent on creativity. Does this idea not go against the spirit of Human Rights Declaration? Yes. If copyright protection is applied rigidly, it can hamper progress of the society. However, copyright laws are enacted with necessary exceptions and limitations to ensure that a balance is maintained between the interests of the creators and of the community.

## THE COPYRIGHT ACT OF 1957

The Copyright Act, 1957 protects original literary, dramatic, musical and artistic works and cinematograph films and sound recordings from unauthorized uses. Unlike the case with patents, copyright protects the expressions and not the ideas. There is no copyright in an idea.

## MEANING OF COPYRIGHT

For the purpose of the Act 'Copyright' means exclusive rights by virtue of and subject to the provisions of the Act the protection provided by copyright to the efforts of writers, artists, designers, dramatists, musicians, architects and producers of sound recordings, cinematograph films and computer software, creates an atmosphere conducive to creativity, which induces them to create more and motivates others to create.

In case of a literary, dramatic or musical work, to do and authorize the doing of any of the following acts;

1. to reproduce the work in any material form;
2. to publish the work;
3. to perform the work in public;
4. to produce, reproduce, perform or publish any translation of the work;
5. to make a cinematographic film or a record in respect of the work;
6. to communicate the work by broadcast; and
7. to make any adaptation of the work.

## WORKS IN WHICH COPYRIGHT SUBSIST

Copyright subsists throughout India in the following classes of works:

Work first published in India;
First published outside India-author is Indian;
Unpublished works- Author is citizen of India;
Original literary, dramatic, musical and artistic works;
Cinematograph films; and
Sound recordings.

*What is a work?*

A work means any of the following:
a literary,
a dramatic, musical or artistic work,
a cinematograph film, or
a sound recording.

*Who is the first owner of copyright in a work?*

Ordinarily the author is the first owner of copyright in a work.

*Who is an author?*

- In the case of a literary or dramatic work the author, i.e., the person who creates the work.

- In the case of a musical work, the composer.
- In the case of a cinematograph film, the producer.
- In the case of a sound recording, the producer.
- In the case of a photograph, the photographer.
- In the case of a computer generated work, the person who causes the work to be created.

## EXCEPTIONS

*Employment*

In the case of a government work, government shall, in the absence of any agreement to the contrary, be the first owner of the copyright therein.

*Contract*

In the case of a work made in the course of the author's employment under a contract of service or apprenticeship, the employer shall, in the absence of any agreement to the contrary, be the first owner of the copyright therein

*What is Copyrightable*

Unpublished manuscript
Lectures
Letters
Questionnaires
Catalogues
Dictionaries, Directories
Slogans
Question papers
Maps
Photographs
Computer software

*What is not copyrightable?*

Historical Facts
Book Titles
Ideas

## PRINCIPLE OF FAIR DEAL

Indian Copyright Act also provides a provision for fair deal. Fair use of a copyright work for research, study, criticism, review and news reporting, as well as use of works in library and schools and in the legislatures, is permitted without specific permission of the copyright owners. In order to protect the interests of users, some exemptions have been prescribed in respect of specific uses of works enjoying copyright. Some of the exemptions are the uses of the work

(i) for the purpose of research or private study;
(ii) for criticism or review;
(iii) for reporting current events;
(iv) in connection with judicial proceeding;
(v) performance by an amateur club or society if the performance is given to a non-paying audience; and
(vi) the making of sound recordings of literary, dramatic or musical works under certain conditions.

*Term of protection of copyright?*

Copyright is not protected in perpetuity. It is protected for a limited period of time. In the case of original literary, dramatic, musical and artistic works the 60-year period is counted from the year following the death of the author. In the case of cinematograph films, sound recordings, photographs, posthumous publications, anonymous and pseudonymous publications, works of government and works of international organizations, the 60-year period is counted from the date of publication.

*Is it necessary to register a work to claim copyright?*

No. It is not mandatory to get the work registered, Acquisition of copyright is automatic and it does not require any formality. However, It is advised. As certificate of registration of copyright and the entries made therein serve as *prima facie* evidence in a court of law with reference to dispute relating to ownership of copyright.

*Procedure for registration of a work under the Copyright Act, 1957*

Copyright comes into existence as soon as a work is created and no formality is required to be completed for acquiring copyright. However, facilities exist for having the work registered in the Register of Copyrights maintained in the Copyright Office of the Department of Education.

The entries made in the Register of Copyrights serve as *prima-facie* evidence in the court of law. The Copyright Office has been set up to provide registration facilities to all types of works and is headed by a Registrar of Copyrights and is located at B.2/W.3, C.R. Barracks, Kasturba Gandhi Marg, New Delhi- 110 003.

Chapter VI of the Copyright Rules, 1956, as amended, sets out the procedure for the registration of a work. Copies of the Act and Rules can be obtained from the Manager of Publications, Publication Branch, Civil Lines, Delhi or his authorized dealers on payment. The procedure for registration is as follows:

(a) Application for registration is to be made on Form IV (Including Statement of Particulars and Statement of Further Particulars) as prescribed in the first schedule to the Rules;
(b) Separate applications should be made for registration of each work;
(c) Each application should be accompanied by the requisite fee prescribed in the second schedule to the Rules; and
(d) The applications should be signed by the applicant or the advocate in whose favour a Vakalatnama or Power of Attorney has been executed. The Power of Attorney signed by the party and accepted by the advocate should also be enclosed.

Each and every column of the Statement of Particulars and Statement of Further Particulars should be replied specifically.

*Assignment of Copyright*

It can be assigned like any other property- rent or Sale

(1) Whole (2) Partial (3) Territorial

## MODE OF ASSIGNMENT

1. *Written:* No assignment of the copyright in any work shall be valid unless it is in writing signed by the assignor or by his/her duly authorized agent.

2. *Extent:* The assignment of the copyright in any work shall, among other things, indicate clearly the rights proposed to be assigned.
3. *Disputes:* In case of any dispute the matter may be referred to the Copyright Board (a quassi judicial body set up by the Government for exclusively dealing with copyright cases). The Board in its own wisdom may decide the case.
4. *Duration:* The period for which the assignment is given.
5. *Territorial Extent:* The geographical areas for which the rights are assigned.
6. *Assignment Fee:* The amount mutually agreed as compensation for the assignment.

*Copyright infringements*

The following are some of the commonly known acts involving infringement of copyright:

(i) Making infringing copies for sale or hire or selling or letting them for hire;
(ii) Permitting any place for the performance of works in public where such performance constitutes infringement of copyright;
(iii) Distributing infringing copies for the purpose of trade or to such an extent so as to affect prejudicially the interest of the owner of copyright ;
(iv) Public exhibition of infringing copies by way of trade; and
(v) Importation of infringing copies into India.

The following acts are not considered an infringement of copyright.

(a) A fair dealing with a literary, dramatic, musical or artistic work for the purposes of:
    (i) research or private study,
    (ii) criticism or review, whether of that work or of any other copyright work.
(b) A fair dealing with a copyright work for the purposes of reporting current events:
    (i) in a newspaper, magazine or similar periodical;
    (ii) computer back up copy for protection against loss of data;
    (iii) reproduction of judicial proceedings for purpose of reporting;

(iv) use of copyright material by a teacher or pupil in the course of instruction;
(v) as part of the questions to be answered in an examination; and
(vi) report of a lecture delivered in public.

## PIRACY

The term piracy means an unauthorized and illegal reproduction or distribution of materials protected by copyright, patent or trademark law. There is no separate law on piracy.It is covered under Indian Penal Pode, 1860;Code of Criminal Procedure ( CRPC) 1973; and, Indian Evidence Act,1872.

*Procedures and Remedies against Piracy*

1. Complaint: File a complaint to the police against the infringement.
2. Court injunction: May file an application for permanent injunction.
3. Raids: Raids can be conducted under the court's order on the bookshop, warehouse, printing press, binder and pirated goods may be destroyed in public.

*Suggestions*

Owner of copyright should not hesitate to file a complaint.

Authors and publishers should be encouraged to register the work with copyright office.

Police should be more active in Intellectual property rights cases.

Piracy should be condemned by the society.

Special courts to deal with intellectual property rights cases should be established.

Penalties should be heavy so that people are discouraged to violate the economic rights of an author.

# 24

# Publisher's Contract

Publishing is a partnership game. The two most important partners in the production of the book are the *author,* who writes the book and the *publisher*, who brings the other partners together and usually serves as the basic taker of business risk of publishing a book.

Both author and publisher work together with one common aim of making new knowledge available to readers. They function in harmony, sometimes in disharmony.

*The Author:* An author is creator of ideas to be given to the world through a book. The author is the owner of right to publish the work he had created. Normally, he tries to sell the right or assign to a publisher to publish the work he has created. If he does not want to share his ideas with the rest of the world, there is nothing that can prevent him from hiding the manuscript away.

*The Publisher:* A Publisher is an integral part of the intellectual and cultural system of any country. Most simply, a publisher is a coordinator of the process by which a book is produced. Publishers have considerable power and influence on what is published and sold.

*The relationship:* Publishers want manuscripts to publish and authors want publishers to publish their works. The relationship is on equal footing. No favours done to either side. A balance, therefore, has to be created and this is done with the help of a balanced contract between the author and publisher for publishing a book. In a model contract, interests of both the parties are taken care of.

## TYPES OF CONTRACTS

A formal contract is not only desirable but also essential for reasons more than one. If the agreement is properly drawn up, it defines in most concise form possibly the nature of the arrangement between the author and the publisher. Agreement between an author and a publisher can be of four kinds, any other form will be a combination of these four kinds.

1. *Outright Purchase of Copyright:* This simply means the purchase of the work after making a lump sum payment after which the author has no right or concern with the profit or sale of the book. This is an exceedingly bad arrangement for the author. Many new aspirant authors, whose books became an instant bestsellers have been victim of 'outright purchase system', only to see their publishers making fortunes because of the author's ignorance.

2. *Profit Sharing Agreement:* It is a partnership venture. No profit is booked till the actual cost of production is recovered by way of sale. The proportion of profit is decided in the beginning. This is also an arrangement, which is tilted towards the publisher.

3. *Commission Agreement:* In this arrangement the author pays the entire cost of production of the book and assumes the liability of costs and owns the stock. The publisher is paid for the professional help for getting the work published. Publisher also receives some commission on the sales. This is also called Vanity publishing.

4. *The Royalty system:* This is one the most commonly used form of agreement. Under this arrangement. A publisher agrees to pay to the author an agreed percentage of royalty on the number of copies sold. The royalty is calculated usually on the printed sale price. Publisher is also supposed to submit a royalty statement once or twice a year. Most contracts, these days, are signed on the basis of royalty system.

## MAIN CLAUSES OF A ROYALTY CONTRACT

1. *Author's Warranty:* Under this clause, an author guarantees that he is the sole author and owner of the book and is legally entitled to assign the publishing rights and that these rights have not been given to any other person before the agreement.

Author also has to undertake that nothing has been stolen or plagiarized and it does not contain anything libelous or obscene and shall be solely responsible in the court of law, if any such thing is found at a later date.

2. *Delivery of manuscript:* Under this clause the author undertakes to deliver the manuscript by an agreed date in a form and condition,

which is reasonably good to be sent to the printer. Failure to do so may result in termination of the contract.

3. *Grant of Right to Publish:* Author also authorizes the publisher to publish the work. This is a sensitive clause and should be explicit in what authority is being given to the publisher. To publish only in one language or one edition only, or in one territory only, etc. This is further discussed in detail under subsidiary rights clause.

4. *Next Literary Work:* A publisher spends a lot of money in promoting an author and his book. Publisher may have to project the author for his future publications. Publisher, therefore, in his own interest, likes that an author to agree that his next literary work will be offered to the publisher first. In other words the publisher shall have the first right to consider the next publication. The details of the future agreement are not mentioned. This, in fact, is a contract within a contract and binds an author to submit his next work to the earlier publisher. This clause is harsh on the author.

5. *Agreement to Publish:* After the author has granted the right to publish his work to the publisher, the publisher further agrees the work within a stipulated period, which is mutually agreed upon. Or within a reasonable time after the receipt of the manuscript. A failure to do so may end up in the break of the contract and author may take back the manuscript.

6. *Royalty Payment:* Under this clause, the publisher agrees to pay to the author the mutually agreed royalty in respect of number of copies sold. The royalty shall be paid on the basis of selling price. No royalty is payable on unsold copies, review, presentation, complimentary or shop soiled copies. The royalty statement shall be submitted once or twice a year as mutually agreed upon. No royalty is paid on copies sold at below the production cost. All the arrangements are mentioned in the contract.

7. *Advance Payment of Royalty:* Publishers, sometimes, to help the author complete the work in time, advance certain amount before the publication of the book. This amount is usually called advance royalty that is adjusted in the royalty payable to the author. No further payment is generally made till the previous advance is exhausted against the royalty due after the book sale.

8. *Other Rights or Subsidiary Rights:* These days the work of an author can be produced in many different formats and forms, besides

the format of a book. These formats and other forms in which the author's work can be presented to the readers are covered under the clause of subsidiary rights.

These rights are separately negotiated and are classified into *Print rights* and *Performing rights.*

*Print Rights*

(i) Reprint rights,
(ii) Translation rights,
(iii) Paperback rights,
(iv) Book club rights,

*Performing rights*

(i) Audio rights,
(ii) Film rights,
(iii) Theatre rights,
(iv) adaptation rights,
(v) Web rights, etc.

It is a practice to give good share to the publisher in use of print rights and author keeps the lion's share in the income from sale or assignment of performing rights. The reason being that any print form may compete with the sale of the original edition.

9. *Free Copies:* The contract also clarifies the number of free copies that will be given to the author and amount of discount, which will be given to the author for purchase of other copies. The author is not supposed to sell these discounted copies.

10. *Manuscripts and proofs:* Though author agrees under the *delivery of manuscript* clause that he shall supply the manuscript in a form which is reasonably good to be sent to the printer, in practice this seldom happens. Not only this, authors keep revising the manuscript till the last stage. This causes a problem for the publishers to bring out the book according to the schedule. The contract provides that the author shall read the proofs and will pay for author's alterations, which he may introduce after the pages, have been set. It is also decided who will prepare the index, if any. If the publisher prepares the index, it is usually charged to the author.

11. *Arbitration:* This is another important clause of the contract. In event of disagreement, of which chances are many, provision is made to arbitrate the dispute. In such an event both author and publisher will choose one arbitrator each of their choice. The two will choose the third one and three will try to resolve the issue of dispute. The parties generally accept the decision, in case the decision of the arbitration is not acceptable, either of the party can go to the court of law for resolving the issue.

12. *Termination of the Contract:* In most cases the contract lasts till the expiry of copyright. In certain conditions, the agreement can be terminated, for example, if the publisher fails to keep his commitment and delays beyond a reasonable limit the publication of the book or lets it go out of print and fails to bring out the reprint edition after expiry of the notice period (usually six months), or the author fails in some of his obligations, the contract can be terminated.

# Index